Advance Praise for Wendy

"Bravo to Wendy Adamson for not only her bravery but for her delicate balance of carefully crafted descriptions mixed with brash inner dialogue. We've all heard about the double lives of PTA moms doing meth but *Mother Load* is the real deal, pulling back the curtain on that so-called perfect domestic life and showing us again that addiction is an evil equal opportunist. Engaging, moving, insightful, *Mother Load* is a must read." — **Amy Dresner**, *author of My Fair Junkie*

* * *

"Every one who either is or knows someone who has been a drug addict, alcoholic, or prescription drug user – and I think that covers all of us – needs to read this book. Wendy gives you an honest and no holds barred insight into one woman's struggles with addiction, and what it took to transform herself into the creative and gifted woman she is today. An amazing and truly inspiring read."
— **Hawk Koch**, *Former President of the Academy of Motion Picture Arts and Sciences, Veteran Movie Producer and Author.*

* * *

"I just learned that Wendy Adamson's book, relating her trajectory from gun-toting, meth-head momma with a sofa-sized chip on her shoulder to gentle, sober therapist, could be on its way to the public. What a boon that will be to both the curious and the recovered. With great humor and humility, she tells how she traveled that road and arrived, scabby but upright. I am breathless with anticipation!"
— **Meredith Baxter** - *Actress, Author, Activist*

* * *

"Wendy Adamson shows us how the human spirit has the infinite ability to heal despite the adverse side effects of childhood trauma. In Mother Load, the reader witnesses one woman's fierce determination to heal the impact left on her children through her own drug addiction by tipping the cosmic scales towards recovery and ultimate good. A raw, inspiring story and one that should be read by anyone who has ever struggled to forgive themselves." — **Paul Hook-Partner-***ICM Partners*

* * *

"Wendy's raw and truthful tale begins with the downward spiral of addiction, a crazed path bent on a dead end. Luckily that struggle brings her to her knees and from there towards the reckoning of recovery. This book is about waking up and living to tell what life is like on the other side."
— **Alex Hedison-Actress** *and Photographer*

MOTHER LOAD

A Memoir of Addiction, Gun Violence
& Finding a Life of Purpose

by Wendy Adamson

ROTHCO PRESS • LOS ANGELES, CALIFORNIA

Published by
ROTHCO PRESS
8033 West Sunset Blvd.
Suite 1022
Los Angeles, CA 90046

Rothco Press is a division of Over Easy Media Inc.

ISBN: 978-1-945436-24-6

"A mother's body against a child's
body makes a place. It says you are here....
Without this body against you, there is no place.
The absence of a body against my body
created a gap, a hole, a hunger.
This hunger determined my life."

-Eve Ensler

Dedicated to Jerry and Rikki.

Contents

Part I

1. Mother Interrupted
2. Got Milk?
3. Sybil Brand Institute for Women
4. Good Morning Ladies
5. Mad Max
6. Phone Home
7. My Day in Court
8. Parenthood
9. Divorce: The Jail House Way
10. The Truth
11. Parenting Class
12. The Smoking Ban
13. Sugar Addict
14. Family Day
15. Self Esteem
16. Roll It Up

Part II

17. The Interview
18. Probation
19. Sober Living
20. Panic Attack
21. Slippery Slope
22. The Room Mate
23. Holey Shoes
24. Holy Shit

25. The Prodigal Son
26. Circling The Drain
27. Boundaries

Part III

28. Mother's Day
29. Surrender To Win
30. The Path Gets Narrower
31. Self Supporting
32. An Apple Falls in My Lap
33. Breaking The Cycle
34. The Scene of The Crime
35. The Sins of The Father
36. The Ripple Effect
37. Where There's Smoke
38. Long Lost Sister
39. Comparing Notes
40. The Family System
41. Brother's Keeper
42. Healing Trauma
43. Crossing Paths
44. Identity Crisis
45. The Artists Way
46. Pixie
47. Full Circle
48. School of Hard Knocks
49. A Family Disease
50. Self-Care
51. The Relapse
52. Amends
53. Letting Go
54. Epilogue

Mother Interrupted

When I looked out the peephole of my front door, Cat, a twenty-four-year-old tweaker, was standing in a cropped t-shirt and skintight jeans, her blond hair covering one eye, peek-a-boo style. She had scored earlier that day and was back for more. It was obvious that she was doing a shit load of meth. But who was I to judge?

It was the early nineties and my husband Max and I were living the so-called American Dream. We had two boys and managed apartment complexes with a swimming pool in a quiet suburb in of Los Angeles. We would go to Disneyland, attend their little league games, participate in the school bake sales and enjoy an occasional Sunday Bar-B-Q. What set us apart from other parents? We were smoking copious amounts of methamphetamine.

Opening the door, a crack, I looked over Cat's shoulder to make sure she wasn't being followed. "Come on in," I said, quickly shutting the door behind her. Our nine-year-old son Rikki had fallen asleep while playing with his GI Joe's in his bedroom. My sixteen-year-old, Jerry who had grown to nearly six feet overnight was staying at his friend's house a few blocks away. I hadn't gotten any real sleep in days and was just about to call it a night when she knocked.

A fringed leather purse bounced off her hip as she sashayed to the couch.

"I like your purse," I said. "Very sixties."

Cat sat down and fondled it like it was a puppy, "Oh this thing? I got it for ten bucks."

"Ten bucks?" I was struck with envy.

"Yes ma'am."

Why does this bimbo refer to me as a ma'am? Is she trying to imply I'm old? How about I smack you upside the head with your puppy purse, you blond dimwit? I flashed her a phony smile.

Just then, Max walked in, shirtless. He had a botched tattoo of my name over his heart and on his right bicep a tattoo that said MOM. He was still in good shape in spite all the drugs we were doing. He was rubbing his jet-black curly hair with a towel.

"Yo, what's happening Cat?"

"Hi Max," she giggled. "I came by to see if it's too late to score a gram?"

The dealer, wanting to cut down on foot traffic, had assigned Max as the middle man and for his efforts he'd get a cut of whatever he bought.

"Giiirrrlll, you know speed freaks don't sleep," he wagged his finger. "It's never too late to score from a meth connection."

Cat laughed, while I blankly stared off in space. I had heard the recycled-speed-freak jokes before, just like I had heard all of Max's jokes. I figured that's just what happens when you're married to someone for twenty years. Everything ends up being old recycled news.

Within minutes Max and Cat headed out the front door to the connections across town. When the coast was clear, I rushed to the master bedroom and pulled out a stash I had tucked away earlier that day. We used to split everything down the middle but due to increasing paranoia, I had convinced myself Max was doing speed behind my back. Besides, by that time I couldn't get enough of it inside me fast enough.

I poured a generous line of the white, glassy powder onto the crease of six-inch-squared-off tinfoil. With a straw gripped in my teeth, I held a flame a few inches underneath. The powder began to smolder and a metallic smoke spiraled upward. I sucked it in like a human vacuum cleaner, determined not to let any of it get away. I held the smoke in my lungs until they felt they might explode.

As I set the foil down my heart was pounding like a drum. I gripped the edge of the mattress, riding the rush of adrenaline like a racecar driver hugging the wall of a sharp turn. The ceiling fan spun overhead. A dog barked somewhere in the neighborhood. The neurons fired in my brain like it was the Fourth of July. My bony chest heaved with my long brown hair falling in my face.

I was as jumpy as a lab rat and wanted to direct the frenetic energy in a constructive manner so, I went to the kitchen, sat on the sticky linoleum floor and started emptying the cabinets of all its pots and pans around me. I was trying to scale back because I had way too much 'stuff'. I mean who needs three cheese graters when I barely use one?

I looked down at the soles of my feet. They were filthy! Deep cracks ran along the edges of my heels. I made a mental note to take a shower but quickly dismissed the idea. The meth always made the water feel like tiny needles shooting all over my body. I shoved a nostril in my arm pit. It smelled like rancid meat. Maybe I'd take a bath later on?

It was hard for me to stay focused on meth. One minute I would want to attend to house-wifey chores and the next I would feel a creative impulse come on. When inspiration hit me there was just no stopping it. I pushed myself up and rushed to the hallway cabinet where I kept my craft supplies. I had everything from dried flowers, beads and embroidery thread to ceramics, paintbrushes, and crayons. When I opened the cabinet a roll of gold ribbon fell to the floor and spun down the hall.

As I stood my brain released an enormous cascade of creative ideas. I felt like such a visionary who could craft anything with my nimble hands. Eventually, I decided to make a colorful Easter bonnet, even though I had an aversion to anything churchy since being kicked out of Catholic school in the ninth grade. I grabbed my trusty glue gun, a batch of yellow silk flowers and a wide brimmed straw hat. With my arms full of supplies I went to the living room to set up a work station.

I spread everything out on the floor when it occurred to me that the Johnny Carson Show was on. Geez. Was it that late already? Looking at the clock I saw it was now past midnight. Holy shit, Max had been gone for over two hours. Drug dealers may not have the best customer service skills, but normally it wouldn't take so long. Worried, I began flipping through worst-case scenarios in my head. What if he had gotten in a car wreck and he was in the emergency room somewhere? Or what if they got busted, and he was sitting in the back of a police car? What then? I didn't have the money to bail him out.

Then it hit me. Call it a hunch, women's intuition or instinct, but I knew down to the marrow of my tweaking bones that Max was cheating on me. In a flash everything slotted into place and made perfect sense. The way Cat giggled at his stupid jokes, the countless trips to the dealer they made, and the way she looked at him when he walked into the room. Why hadn't I seen it sooner? How could I have been so fucking stupid!

A tightness gripped my chest. I couldn't breathe. I wanted to throw something, hit something with my fist. I wanted to scream at him, "You can't do this to me you fucking asshole!" Instead, I went to the bedroom and smoked some more speed. My hands shook as I sucked the spiraling metallic smoke into my lungs. My jaw clenched so hard it was a wonder my molars didn't turn to dust. How could he do this to me? Hadn't I given him children along with the best years of my life? In that moment it never occurred to me that I could leave or kick him out of the house. Instead, I decided to scare the shit out of him because that way he'd think twice about cheating on me again. I slipped into the closet and stood on my tippy-toes, reaching around until I found the gun at the back of the shelf. My fingers gripped the hard steel of the .38 Smith & Wesson as I pulled it out. Max and I bought the gun a while back from a tweaker who needed cash. We somehow convinced ourselves it was a good idea to have around for protection in case anyone tried to break into our home.

I went to the living room and placed the .38 on top of the armoire. Waiting, I paced back and forth like a feral cat. Images of Max and Cat fucking in the back of her El Camino played inside my brain like bad porno. *Mother fucker!* my head screamed, *you can't do this to me. I cooked your food. I washed your dirty drawers. For what? To be discarded like some old coat you don't want anymore? No fucking way. I won't have it!*

I pushed the screen door, stepped onto the front porch but, there was still no sign of them. My thoughts were coming at me like the rapid fire of an AK-47. He promised me he would never leave me. We were supposed to grow old together. Why hadn't I seen it sooner. How long had it been going on? He can't do this to me. I won't let him.

My heart hammered against my chest. Sweat dripped down my back. My thin t-shirt was clinging to my skin. I had managed to work myself into an eyeball-boiling rage. I looked out the door again, and that's when I saw them. Max was driving her white El Camino, looking for a parking space. I grabbed the .38, barreled through the screen door and ran into the middle of the street. Taking a military stance, behind them, I extended both my arms, with the gun in a two-fisted grip, I aimed above the car and pulled the trigger.

POW!

The sound felt like it reverberated through my chest. The noise was so piercing it's a wonder I didn't give myself permanent hearing damage. The car didn't stop so I ran after it with both my legs and arms pumping away. I distinctly remember seeing my neighbor, Mrs. Brown, peering out her large bay window with her head bobbing back and forth.

Mind your own business you nosy bitch. This is a domestic affair.

When they turned the corner, I darted in between two parked vehicles and caught my foot on the curb. I fell onto the wet grass but popped back up like one of those blow up dolls that won't stay down. When I turned the corner, I was shocked to find the El Camino sitting in the middle of the street. I rushed over like a deranged special ops commando and hurled my torso across the still warm hood. My chest heaved. I was panting like a dog in heat. Cat was sitting shotgun. I pointed the gun directly at Max's face. His big brown eyes filled with terror. It was a look I'd never seen before. Those were the same soulful eyes I'd fallen in love with at sixteen years old. He was the love of my life. My best friend. The father of my children.

In an instant it felt like I slipped out of my body and was staring down at myself sprawled out across the hood of the car. I heard a voice of reason inside my head say, "You know, Wendy, if someone were to see you right now they might think you were crazy." And they would have been absolutely right. I was in the middle of a drug-induced psychotic break. Sleep deprived and smoking way too much methamphetamine for any human being to consume, I had snapped. I had lost my mind just like my mother had years before.

Then Max must have come to his senses because he stepped on the gas. As the car moved forward I slid off the hood and landed solidly on my feet. Pointing the gun downward so I wouldn't hit anybody, I fired another round. As I did Cat's face contorted... *Oh shit! Did I hit her? No way! The gun was pointed down.*

Out of breath, I watched the taillights disappear with the weapon dangling by my side. That was not at all what I had hoped to achieve. My next thought was to change my clothes so no one could identify me in a lineup if the cops happened to show up.

I ran back to the house but before I went inside, I shoved the gun under a pile of dead leaves by the back porch.

Once inside I checked on Rikki, who was still asleep. As I stood watching him breathe one would think his innocence would penetrate my drug-induced state but that was not the case. It was as if the meth, a diuretic, had not only leached my sanity, but drained my maternal instincts as well.

I headed for the bedroom where I caught sight of my reflection in the mirror. My breath nearly jackknifed. My brown hair was disheveled, the bones in my face were all sharp edges and I was hunched over. My eyes were like two dead, vacant pools and my skin was a sallow gray. It was jarring how much I looked like my mother had when she had gone insane.

A familiar darkness grabbed me like fingers around my throat. I wanted to stop the madness but had no idea how.

I flinched when I heard some noise outside. I opened the front door and when I stepped onto the porch I was blinded by a dozen spotlights, pointing at me like fingers of accusation. "Hands in the air!" a disembodied voice yelled from beyond the glare.

The Catholic girl still residing in me did exactly what she was told as a stampede of Lomita sheriffs surrounded me. It all happened fast after that. One of them cuffed my hands while another patted me down and others rushed inside the apartment.

My legs shook like a high-strung Chihuahua. A scruffy-looking cop slipped plastic baggies over my hands and manila envelopes over that.

"What's going on? What, what what are you doing?" I asked, feigning innocence.

A young cop secured the envelopes around my wrists. with duct tape.

"My son is asleep in there…"

A cop yelled inches from my face. "SHUT UP!"

I flinched. I felt like I might pass out.

When they were done, it looked like I had two flippers where my hands were supposed to be. A young sheriff led me by my arm, shoved me into the back seat of his squad car and slammed the door. I leaned my forehead against the window and watched as cops scurried in and out of my apartment. Where was Max? Why hadn't he come back to see what was going on? What was going to happen to me? I needed a cigarette so fucking bad.

I looked down at the strange appendages resting on my lap. I realized the cops were trying to keep the gunpowder intact on my hands as evidence. I gripped the corner of the envelope with my teeth and began ripping, tearing, spitting the scraps of paper on the floor. I was like a trapped animal determined to get free. Finally, I broke through the plastic baggies and started licking my hand and fingers. I was no dummy. I knew how to outsmart those cops. I was in a frenzy when the front door of the squad car flew open. A good-looking cop peered through the thick mesh screen.

"Look, Wendy." He paused. "Why don't you just tell me where you put the gun? It will be easier for you if you cooperate with us."

"Under the leaves by the back porch." The words just rolled right off my tongue. You clearly wouldn't want to drop me behind enemy lines. He ran off like a school kid picked for the winning team. When I thought about Jerry and Rikki my heart sank to my feet.

Oh God, oh God, oh God, oh God oh shit shit shit. My poor, poor boys. What the fuck have I done?

Got Milk?

Mommy was sick, crazy sick. I felt her insanity long before I had any name for it. I was five-years old and Mommy was dressed in a printed, A-line skirt with a pink tailored blouse tucked in at the waist. Her red pumps clicked against the linoleum floor. She was pretty, with delicate features, a long elegant neck, and her brown hair cut in a fashionable bob.

I had stayed home sick that day from kindergarten while my two brothers and sister were at school. Mommy had cut my brown hair but she had cut the bangs crooked. I thought they looked stupid but she said, not to worry they would grow out fast. As I waited I anxiously tore bits of napkin into thin strips as I sat at the breakfast nook. Mommy was making me a peanut butter and grape jelly sandwich on my favorite Wonder Bread. I was hungry and wanted to eat.

All of the sudden she froze staring inside the open refrigerator. I watched her, sensing something was wrong. My heart rate accelerated. The generator kicked on and a rush of cold air hit my face.

"Mommy?"

She didn't answer. My stomach tightened in a ball.

"Mommy, are you okay?"

"Shut up!" she snapped.

Mommy grabbed a bottle of milk in each of her hands, muttering scary things. "The milkman is trying to poison us all." She started pouring the liquid down the sink.

My heart was racing. I was fighting the urge to run but where would I go? Besides she would just catch me and that would make things worse. I tried a different approach. "Mommy the milkman is a nice man," reassuring her, but my idea didn't work.

Slamming a bottle down on the counter, it sent shards of glass across the black and white checkered floor. Then my Mommy whipped around and glared at me. I swore it felt like something evil had crawled up inside her and was watching me from behind her eyes. I sank down low and grabbed the edge of the table with my hands in a pointless effort to hold on. Mommy rushed over, snatched me by my arms like a rag-doll and with incredible force dropped me to the floor.

"Mommy, Mommy … please don't," I sobbed.

"You are a bad girl," her voice deep. "A very bad girl."

Clutching my elbows from behind, Mommy pushed me out in front of her like a shopping cart. Every few steps she thrust her knee between my shoulder blades. I pleaded for her to stop but it was like she couldn't hear me.

She pushed me into my bedroom. "Don't come out or you'll be sorry." Mommy slammed the door.

Hurling myself onto my bed and burrowing under the covers, I clutched my knees to my chest and curled up into a tight ball. Mommy terrified me. I knew something was gravely wrong with her and I thought it was something I did. She made me feel so small. So insignificant and I hated her for that. "I wish you would die Mommy… I wish you'd go away and never come back."

Sybil Brand Institute for Women

T he black and white county bus rolled into the enclosed parking lot of Sybil Brand, Women's Central Jail, located just East of Los Angeles. Looped razor-wire ran along the top of the eight-foot wall. It had been eight years since I had done time there for petty theft and other drug related charges. I had sworn back then I would never return. But my life was nothing more than a vicious cycle of me repeating the same mistakes over and over again with no idea why. As the bus jerked to a stop the air brakes released with a loud hissing sound. A female Sheriff hopped on the bus with a dark ponytail swinging behind her like a pendulum.

"ALRIGHT LADIES, LISTEN UP," she yelled. "If you're a returnee, get your county clothes and go back to your dorms. All you fish (as in, fish out of water) — LINE UP OUT HERE IN ONE SINGLE LINE."

All the women stood up at once and poured into the narrow aisle of the bus. Putrid body odor clung to the air as strangers pressed together like cattle inching toward their slaughter. I steadied myself with my hand on the back of a seat. When I moved forward my joints felt like unoiled pistons. With the drugs leaving my system it seemed like my knees could buckle beneath me any moment. Once I stepped outside onto the pavement I had to blink several times to adjust to the afternoon light.

I flinched at the sound of a loud metallic clang. The barred gate rolled open in front us and we were ushered into a chamber. Once everyone was inside, the gate behind us slammed shut pinning us in like animals.

Sybil Brand was even more run down than before. The bars were chipped with layers of green and yellow paint. The gray walls had brown smudges running along the sides. The years of repression, sweat and fear hung in the air like a toxic cloud. I'm pretty sure I wasn't the only one in there who wanted to die.

Another gate opened to my left and a short, boxy officer with thick glasses beckoned me with a curled finger to the adjacent room. She led me to a counter to sign paperwork.

"You'll need to take that ring off," she pointed at my wedding band.

"It doesn't come off."

I didn't want to relinquish the ring. It was the only evidence I had that someone actually loved me outside those gray walls. But I couldn't even be sure of that anymore.

She dumped a glob of what looked like axle-grease into my hand. "This will help."

I smeared it around my ring finger and tugged again. "I'm telling you it doesn't come off."

Her forehead creased in frustration as she handed me a paper towel. "Alright. Never mind." Admissions ran on a tight schedule so she must have decided it wasn't worth getting in a power struggle.

Next she put a white band with my name and booking number around my wrist. It looked like the ones they put on patients in hospitals. With a tool that resembled a hole puncher she secured the grommets. "This is your identification so whatever you do, don't take it off."

After the initial paperwork, I was ushered into a dingy holding tank. A girl was sitting in the corner crying with hair hanging in her face. A prostitute in a red mini-skirt was pacing, her high-heels click-clacking across the floor. The cell was littered with cigarette butts. Partially eaten cheese and bologna sandwiches were thrown in the corner. I sat down on the cold concrete slab and cupped my forehead in my hands. I pushed back the tears telling myself. Don't cry. Don't cry. I was afraid if I showed any emotions, other than anger, it would be taken as a sign of weakness. I had to be strong even though I felt like I was going to die. I didn't know if Max loved me anymore or was it finally over?

I couldn't fathom going on without him. A stone felt lodged in the back of my throat. An old familiar ache was crushing me on the inside.

My thoughts kept traveling back to that dreaded night when I was waiting for Max to get home. I thought about the many ways I could have handled it differently. I could have had a conversation with him. But no. I always screwed things up. I thought about my Rikki and Jerry again. What did they think of their poor mother who was locked away? I wanted to talk to them and tell them how sorry I was for everything. To tell them, just as soon as I get this mess straightened out, I'd be back home. My mind was entrenched in denial which was made it even harder to come to terms with reality.

After another torturous hour, an officer with short, spikey red hair opened the door and called me out. I was taken to a small room where she rolled each of my fingers in ink before transferring my prints onto index cards. Afterwards, I was escorted to the showers, a brightly-lit, tiled room where I joined other women who were already waiting there. The smell of bleach and disinfectant was so strong it seemed like it could singe the hairs inside the nostrils.

"Alright ladies put all your clothes into the bins on the floor," Red yelled.

I hated this part of the booking process but I didn't have a choice, so I pulled my t-shirt over my head and dropped it into the bin. The jeans I had been wearing felt like they were glued to my skin as I peeled them off my thin, spindly legs. Once I was completely undressed, I looked like a Holocaust survivor. My ribs jutted out like a corrugated washboard. My stomach looked as if it was carved out with a knife. When I glanced down at myself it was as if I was seeing my body for the first time. The drugs had clearly distorted my perception. Embarrassed, I crossed my arms in front of my chest as shame slithered up my spine.

All of the sudden Red was directly in my face. "Open your mouth," she said.

My oral hygiene had suffered because I never wanted to undergo a dentist's drill while tweaking on meth. As a result, my once perfect teeth had cavernous black holes. As Red shined her flashlight into my mouth and told me to lift my tongue I felt exposed. Her head tilted back and forth as she shined the light on my neglected teeth. When she moved onto the next inmate, I let out a long sigh.

A weathered inmate walked down the line with an industrial sized bottle. The inmates helped in all the daily operations of the jail and were referred to as trustees.

"Open your hand," she said.

She squirted a thick amber solution in my palm.

"What's this for?" an inmate asked.

Red stood in front with her hands on her hips. "We don't want any of you ladies smuggling critters into our jail so wash your hair and pubic area with this shampoo," she said.

The showers went on behind us. "Alright ladies step inside."

I got under the barely warm stream of water and shivered hard. The least they could do was give us hot water. I rubbed the solution into my tangled hair that hadn't seen a comb for days. Some of it dripped down my forehead burning my eyes. My teeth chattered loudly.

Red was pacing and yelling outside the shower stalls, "Hurry up ladies. We don't have all night."

The water shut off whether you were done or not. I got out and stood on the thin paper the size of a place mat. The trustee handed each of us a stiff white towel. Trembling, I patted my goose-bumped flesh. My tangled hair was in desperate need of some conditioner, a comb…or a hair-dryer perhaps?

Fuck, I want to go home. I want to hug Jerry and Rikki. I want to take them in my arms ant tell them how sorry I am for screwing everything up.

As we stood on the mats naked, we were doused under the arms and between the legs with a toxic bug spray. After that, Red was standing directly in front of me barking orders she probably had said a thousand times before. "Run your fingers through your hair! Lift your arms. Turn around and let me see the bottom of your feet! Bend over. Spread your cheeks. Now squat. Let me hear you cough!"

With Red's last command I could sense her beady eyes peering up my vagina. Lucky for me, no crack pipes or syringes flew out and she moved on to the next inmate.

When booking was finally over, I was issued a roll-up that consisted of bedding, a gray blanket, a nightgown and a stiff blue county dress.

"Report to dorm 7200 at the end of the hall to the left. An officer will be waiting for you there." Red handed me a hall pass.

Freezing, I shuffled along in plastic slippers through the corridor. I went all the way down the hall until I was met by another sheriff. "Let me see your wristband," she said.

After checking my name with her flashlight she told me my bunk number and unlocked the door.

Once inside I quietly passed the lumps of snoring women. My bunk was all the way in the back against the wall. I slipped the sheet on over the plastic mattress and spread out the wool blanket over that.

When I finally laid down I tried to close my eyes but I couldn't sleep. The regrets consumed me. Regret for what I had done and for what I could have done differently. Regret for how I had wasted my entire life. And the biggest regret of all, for all the hurt I caused my boys. I had failed miserably as a mother. I had failed as a wife. I had failed as a human being. I was a loser and a jury of my peers couldn't convince me otherwise. I pulled the blanket over my head and muffled my cries so no one else could hear me. My mind was a fractured kaleidoscope of images as memories took me back to when I was a kid.

1960

Dressed in a plaid shift, I was playing jacks on the sidewalk when Daddy pulled up in his brand new shiny, black and white convertible Buick.

"Wendy, come here," he yelled, from the driver's seat. I knew Daddy had on his leg-brace he wore ever since early onset of polio and didn't want to get out of the car if he didn't have to.

"Hi Daddy." My seven year old self leaned into the passenger window.

Daddy had a thin mustache that looked like little black wings. Sometimes when he smiled I thought it might fly right off his face. He was wearing his work uniform—a short-sleeved white shirt, a pen holder, and baggy pants held up by a thin black belt. I remember the belt because whenever I was bad he'd whip my bare butt until it was crisscrossed with ribbons of red welts.

"Hey Pooh, how about you and I go to Mel's and grab some lunch?"

"Really, Daddy?" I jumped up and down.

"Come on, get in."

I pulled open the passenger door with both hands and hopped inside. Odors of stale smoke and Old Spice filled the air. It was Daddy's day smell, the smell that hid the vodka and Camel cigarette smoke of the night before.

"I snuck away from work just so we could hang out," he said.

"I like hanging out with you Daddy."

On the drive to Mel's, he started singing along to the radio in his low, smoky-voice. Daddy had a soothing tone when he sang but when he was angry, his voice sounded like it could tear the flesh right off the bone.

We pulled into the semi-circular parking lot and Daddy stopped and turned off the engine. I loved Mel's because you could eat in your car. I pulled on the hairs of my arm until a blond girl with a ponytail came over to the driver's side. Daddy ordered two cheeseburgers, French fries, and two cherry Cokes, which she promptly scratched on her pad before disappearing inside.

We listened to top-forty songs being pumped out of the dashboard speaker. Daddy would tell me the names of each hit song and who was singing it. He knew everybody because he used to be a DJ back in the day.

When the tray of food finally arrived, it was secured onto the driver's window. The burgers were wrapped in a thin yellow sheet of paper, like someone had tucked them into bed. I took a bite and a stream of Thousand Island dressing dripped down my chin. I was slurping up the last of my cherry Coke when Daddy reached over and turned the radio off. He had a serious look on his face.

"Can you keep a secret, Pooh?" he asked.

"Yes Daddy, I love secrets."

"I don't want you telling Bruce, you hear me?"

My younger brother was a pain in the butt so I didn't have a problem keeping a secret from him.

"I promise Daddy," I said, crossing a finger over my heart.

"Your Mommy had a heart attack. She... she died..... and won't be coming home." He wasn't showing the emotions of a man who had just lost his wife. His face was unreadable and I had no idea what this meant.

My breath froze inside my chest. Mommy went away a lot but she always came back. I just thought the hospital would fix her one day and we'd have a normal mother-daughter relationship.

The sweet smell of catsup suddenly made me want to throw up. A narrow shaft of light came through the windshield burning the skin on my arm. I studied Daddy, trying to crawl inside his brain. What was going on with him? All I could think about were their ugly fights and maybe he was happy she was gone.

Another part of me wanted to be held. To be comforted. I wanted my father to tell me everything was going to be all right. But all he said was he had to get back to work. I stared in silence as his tanned hand turned the key of the ignition on.

Moments later he dropped me off at the house, he held a finger to his lips, "Remember Pooh, this is our little secret."

I watched as his shiny car disappeared into a speck down the road. In my plaid dress and black and white Oxford shoes I felt so incredibly small. It felt like he had just pulled the pin out of a grenade and handed it to me. When I turned I saw Tommy playing across the street and ran over to him grabbing him by his arms, "My mommy is dead."

I saw confusion in his pale blue eyes.

"My mommy is dead!" I said it again louder.

He shimmied out of my grip and ran inside his house. Well, he wasn't much help. I looked around and saw Susie bouncing a red rubber ball and ran up to her.

"My mommy's dead."

Her ball rolled away. "What did you say...?"

"I said, my mommy's dead."

Susie frowned and ran off to retrieve her ball.

I would end up telling every kid I found playing on the street that day. In hindsight, I think I was looking for a gesture, an expression or some type of sign that would show me how I should respond after the loss of a mother. I had another secret-a secret I would keep down in the tiny temple of my soul. I thought I killed my mother all those times I had wished that she were dead. I was the one who put the contract out on her life and God had fulfilled the contract. It was probably around that time that the steel vault closed around my heart as I banished any sort of God from my life.

Good Morning Ladies

At five a.m. the fluorescent lights flickered to life. It took a moment to get my bearings but, it all came back to me when I heard an inmate cursing and slamming a locker door. A sickening shiver ran up my spine. I was in withdrawal and every cell in my body screamed for drugs. I covered my eyes with my hand trying to beat back the tsunami of grief that threatened to rise up from within.

"LISTEN UP LADIES," a voice squawked from the PA system. "LINE IT UP FOR BREAKFAST."

It was hard to imagine how I would function amongst all those strange women. Hard to imagine how I would be able to converse. But I knew that no one was allowed to stay in the dorm during meals, so I had to get up. My feet hit the cold concrete floor causing my battered body to shiver hard. I stood up and my head started to swirl like a bowl of water. I grabbed onto the empty bunk on top and lowered my chin to get blood flowing to the brain before the darkness took me down. When the spinning stopped I was able to slip on my county blue dress.

In jail women's dresses were color-coded to signify where you belonged. For instance, a kitchen worker might sport purple, while yellow meant you worked in the laundry room. This way officers could easily detect someone who had wandered out of their area. The women were brought in by different police departments throughout Los Angeles. Most of us were waiting for trial or sentencing but about one-third of the women had already been convicted on charges and were serving their time.

I summoned my scrawny legs to move one foot in front of the other. I felt like the bride of Frankenstein as I shuffled to the bathroom. There was a beehive of activity as women rushed to get ready for breakfast. When one of the six stalls opened up I slipped inside. As I relieved myself my urine reeked of ammonia. I knew it was sign that my liver was working hard to expel all the drugs I had been doing. When I stood back up I had to hold on to the stall to keep from falling over.

Women had started lining up on the other side of the dorm, so I made my way over there. As I approached a shapeless woman with coffee bean skin narrowed her eyes. I quickly looked away. Detoxing, I felt weak and vulnerable.

Many of the women who cycled through the system had a certain look on their faces. Sometimes it was a blank stare. Sometimes it was a look of extreme pain or even anger. The look may be a by-product of losing ones freedom over and over again. Perhaps it comes from all the demoralization endured while locked-up. Or perhaps the look appeared way before that. Perhaps it came as a result of horrific childhood abuse. Maybe it came from not having parents who would protect them when they were kids. I am familiar with that look because I had seen it on my own face many times. And as I gazed at the women in the line, I saw it on theirs. But when I turned my head, another woman came prancing up behind me. She had an athletic build, a ponytail, and for some reason she didn't have the look.

"You came in last night." She smiled big.

"I got in while everyone was asleep." My voice was weak.

"I know. I saw you come in."

I cringed when I thought she might have heard me crying under my blankets the night before. In jail it was critical to be in control of your emotions at all times. I looked away.

"What are you in for?" she asked.

That was the first question everybody seemed to want to know. Sort of like the sixties when people asked you what your astrological sign was. In the past I had charges such as petty theft or under-the-influence which ranked low in prison hierarchy as it were. But now I had a bad ass felony that could earn me a fair amount of instant jailhouse cred.

"Assault with a deadly weapon." Just saying it out loud made it more real.

Amused, she leaned her head to one side, "Who did you assault?"

"Well, ah, ah… my husband was cheating on me."

Her arched eyebrow formed a question mark. "You shot your husband?"

A few heads in front of us turned to eavesdrop.

"No, no. I shot his mistress… but it was an accident. I was really just trying to scare them is all."

She laughed out loud. "That would scare the holy shit out of me alright."

I changed the subject. "What are you in for?"

"Oh, just some run of the mill embezzlement charges." She shrugged.

I would later learn she had been arrested for a massive bank scam and not so run of the mill. In fact, it had made the front page news.

The door opened in front of us and the line inched forward.

"My name is Susan by the way. My bunk is across from you."

"I'm Wendy," I whispered. "Nice to meet you."

As the women spilled out into the corridor we lined up in single file with our shoulders against the wall. Two khaki-clad officers, one in the front and one in the back shouted. "Alright ladies move it."

As I walked it felt like I had lead weights strapped to both my ankles. Within a matter of moments, it felt like I had already run a marathon. I reached my hand up to the wall for support.

"Are you all right?" Susan whispered from behind me.

"I'm dope sick," I said, under my breath.

Susan placed a gentle hand on my shoulder. The gesture alone caused a golf-ball sized lump to form in the back of my throat. It had been so long since anyone had been kind to me. I never expected it to come from behind the walls of Sybil Brand. What I didn't know that first day, was Susan and I would become extremely close. And obviously, this was a time in my life when I could really use a friend.

Mad Max (1968)

At fifteen, my friend Lisa and I were looking for relief from the usual skull-crushing boredom of adolescents who had nothing to do. We sat on the railing of the Santa Monica pier, smoked cigarettes and watched the procession of girls in bikinis and boys in board shorts stroll by. On the sand below us, were sunbathers speckled across the beach with their families in tow.

Sweat dripped down my back under my long brown hair. I could smell the hot dogs and mustard from the food stand across the way. The carousel cranked out organ music, surrounding us in a cloud of sound. I pulled on the frayed threads of my cut-off jeans as I swung my tanned legs back and forth.

All of the sudden my eyes landed on Max, a gorgeous Latino boy who I knew only by reputation. I froze as he swaggered towards us. He was smoking hot, bare chested, hip hugger jeans and a white t-shirt tucked in his back pocket. My muscles tightened. My heart raced like a trapped bird was caught inside my chest.

"Hey Max, what's happening?" Lisa said, puffing out her chest.

Even though Lisa constantly complained about her size D breasts she certainly knew how to use them with the guys. I, on the other hand, felt inadequate because I could barely fit into a beginners bra.

Max gave me a quick smile, but painfully shy, I could barely meet his gaze. The two of them talked easily to one another while I sat there feeling awkward. I stared at Max's stunning features. He had high cheekbones, big brown eyes and black wavy hair. The tips of his long lashes seemed to reach clear to the sky, while I needed heaps of mascara just to see mine.

"Lisa aren't you going to introduce us?" Max gave a taut nod of the head toward me.

"Oh, I thought you two already knew each other." Lisa hated sharing the attention of boys with anyone. "This is Wendy."

Max turned toward me, "How come we've never met before?"

"Different schools maybe?" I said, nerves jangling.

"Where do you go?"

"Santa Monica High."

"I go to Garfield," he said.

Garfield Continuation was where all the bad boys went. It made me like him even more.

You got an extra cigarette on you?" he asked.

I pulled out a crumpled pack of Marlboro's from my back pocket. I fished inside the pack and handed him one. I was about to light up when Max gently took the matches from my hand. Our skin accidentally touched. My face got all hot. My stomach clenched.

He scratched the match and cupped it with one hand while I leaned over and met his offered flame. His thick furry forearm brushed my bare leg. I distinctly remember the surge of energy coming from between my thighs.

"Could I get your phone number Wendy?" he talked from behind blue swirling smoke. "Maybe we could get together sometime?"

My heart beat even faster. "Sure," I said.

Blood rushed through my veins as he pulled out a pen from his back pocket. I recited my number and he scribbled it on his palm. Up until then, a boy had never asked me out on a date. They usually just wanted to fool around so they could tell all their friends about how they got to second or third base with you. But Max seemed different than other guys.

"I'll give you a call," Max said, before he turned to leave.

"Well he clearly likes you," Lisa said, her voice tinged with bitterness.

"You think so?"

"Obviously," she snarled.

While I wanted to believe he did, before Max had slipped into the crowd I convinced myself that someone as gorgeous as that could never like someone as broken as me.

* * *

Later, when I got home, Dad was sitting in his recliner nursing a vodka on the rocks in front of the television. Dad had a flat top with a patch of gray in the front. His brow furrowed when I came into the room. "Where've you been?" he snapped.

My internal defenses flipped up. "At the beach with Lisa."

By this time my relationship with my father had become saturated with bitterness. It had been two years since Irene, our old housekeeper had dropped the bomb. Irene had a sweeping lower chin, and a shock of bright red-orange hair and she loved to drink. One night, Dad had gone out on a date when Irene told me she wanted to talk. As I sat across from her at the dining room table I could tell she was already buzzed. Her pudgy fingers scissored the cigarette as she let out a quick puff of smoke.

"I think it's time you know the truth about your mother Wendy." She sounded like she had marbles in her mouth.

"What are you talking about Irene?"

Just mentioning my mother made my stomach coil up in a knot. No one ever talked about her in our house. To hear Irene invoking her name stirred something old and dark inside of me.

Irene glared with her glassy, red-rimmed eyes. "Your mom killed herself."

"Wha? What do you mean?" I stammered.

"She committed suicide."

"But Dad said it was a heart attack."

"He was just trying to protect you. He thought you were too young to know the truth."

All of the sudden the veil of deception was ripped away. Everything I had been questioning about my mother, suddenly made sense. In that moment I knew her suicide was the reason we never went to her funeral. I knew it was why dad had moved us out of our old neighborhood after she died. I knew it was why we had lost contact with all my cousins and my grandparents on my mother's side. Dad apparently, had taken us into his self-imposed exile in an attempt to keep us from finding out the truth. I felt betrayed. Angry. Livid. I hated him for that.

Now, two years later, my resentments could not be contained whenever we were in the same room.

"Well you need to check in and let me know where you're at." Dad had to have the last word.

"Yeah. Whatever…" I said, before slipping into the bedroom that I shared with my older sister, Diane, who was never home. At least in my room I could escape dad and my two brothers who I wanted nothing to do with.

Later that evening I found myself listening to sad, love songs on my bed while staring at the ceiling. I was depressed and often entertained thoughts of killing myself. I don't know if the suicidal ideation was the result of normal teenage angst or the result of having a mother who had killed herself. All I know is there was dark cloud that hovered over me that wasn't being addressed.

As I laid there sinking into a deep hole of self-pity the phone rang. I picked it up and when I heard Max's voice coming from the other end, my heart leaped clear to my throat. I sat straight up.

We must have talked for two hours that night. I twirled the extension cord around my finger and gazed out the window. I had been praying for a knight in shining armor and when he asked me if I'd go to a Halloween party with him, I couldn't believe my ears. What Max didn't know yet, I would have gone anywhere with him just to get away from my fucked up family.

* * *

The plan was to meet Max at his friend Abel's house on the night of the party. I got dressed up as a gypsy with a long skirt, big silver hoop earrings and a paisley scarf tied around the top of my head. When I looked in the mirror, my brain told me I was ugly, fat and no one would ever want someone as pathetic as me. Obviously, I suffered from an overwhelming sense of self-hatred. Even my own reflection could cause me to cringe.

Later, when I knocked on the door my heart was racing. Max answered dressed like a hooker, with a black wig, tight blue sweater and fake boobs he had made with his mom's bra stuffed with socks. I cracked up when I saw him.

"What's so funny?" He jutted out a hip.

"The way you're dressed."

"Five dolla baby, I make you feel real, real good." I was laughing when he grabbed my wrist, pulled me in and planted a kiss on my lips. My knees felt like they could easily buckle. I had absolutely no defense or boundaries with him. I had never been openly desired by any guy and it was a major boost to my low self-esteem.

He whispered in my ear, "How about a little wine?"

"Okay," I said, wanting to get a buzz on as quickly as possible.

Max handed me a chilled, strawberry wine cooler. I raised it to my mouth and kissed it with my cherry flavored lip-gloss. My long brown hair inched down my back as I tilted the bottle towards the sky. As soon as the liquid crept down my throat, a warmth filled my entire chest. The sensation of heat took my breath away. My brain, a finely tuned torture device, became silent. Alcohol gave me the ability to slip into a different skin. It not only took away my depression, it gave me confidence. Simply put, alcohol helped me to be in this world.

Max eyed me hungrily. I lowered my head. Not wasting time he took me by the hand to the spare room and closed the door behind us. He kissed me again on the mouth with his soft pillowy lips. We pressed against each other. His hard body made me quiver inside. Our breath came in short, quick gasps. He slipped a hand inside my blouse and held my small breast. I shivered hard like a cat. There was such an urgency between us that I had never felt before. If it wasn't for Abel knocking on the door we'd probably have made love right then.

"We're going to be late to the party," Abel yelled from the other side of the door.

We giggled like two school kids as I buttoned up my blouse. "Be right out!" Max yelled.

Once in the living room Max introduced us. Abel was adorable, with a round baby face and the thick body of a linebacker. Abel was dressed like a priest with a white collar and flowing, black robes.

"Want a hit?" he smiled holding out a joint.

I took it from his fingers. As I inhaled the seeds crackled and popped. It was strong and I started to cough.

Abel made the sign of the cross and bowed his head. "Panama Red, such a sacred herb," he said.

I laughed.

A few minutes later we were piling into Abel's pimped out metallic green 1970 Chevy Van with swivel seats, shag carpet and a feathered roach clip that hung from the rear-view mirror.

When we got to the party it was already in full swing. It was a brown stucco house with the garage door wide open. People were in the driveway, on the lawn and some even spilled out into the street. A girl dressed in a cat costume held her tail in one hand as she leaned against some guy who was dressed in a cop uniform. After parking, we were walking up the path, when a friend of Max's yelled, "How much for a blow job?"

"Five dollars, bayyybeee." Max who loved to clown around, pushed out his breasts and pursed his lips.

As we entered the party the speakers were blasting Santana, singing Got Your Spell on Me Baby.. so loud it made my chest vibrate. The first thing I noticed was an elaborate aquarium with emerald green lights and colorful tropical fish darting in and out of a sunken ceramic ship. Abel took off in one direction while Max held me by the hand, snaking us through the crowd. We went straight into the kitchen, which according to Max, was the best room to be in at any party. We scooted into a maroon vinyl booth that had white stuffing leaking from its cracks. I already had a good buzz going when Max got me a wine spritzer and grabbed himself a beer.

Max held court as everyone came over to talk to him. He would make sure to introduce me to all his friends and being that he was so popular he had a lot of them. I didn't know anybody there that night because I had always been very shy. But when I was with Max everybody was so friendly and nice to me. I was beaming with pride. Being with Max made me feel like I had finally arrived. I don't know how much time had passed or how much I drank before the room started to spin. I leaned over and whispered in Max's ear. "I don't feel so good." I thought I was going to throw up.

"Let's get out of here." He helped me up.

I was dizzy when Max led me back through the living room and our hands came loose from one another. But when I turned around to look for Max there was a red headed cowboy who had slipped in between us. I was stunned when the cowboy grabbed a handful of my ass.

"What the hell are you doing?" I yelled, pushing his hand away.

I saw rage flash across Max face who was directly behind him. In an instant Max leaped up and his wig went flying in the other direction. He landed on the cowboy's back and took him down.

The party goers realized there was a fight and the crowd parted like the Red Sea. I was horrified as the two guys rolled across the floor. Piercing screams could be heard as the lights went on. Before I knew it, Max straddled the cowboy and was pummeling him with his fists. I wanted to do something. But how could stop these two angry guys? I took a step back.

After less than a minute Max pushed himself up, one of his boobs had dropped clear to his waist. The cowboy should have stayed down but instead, he sprung back up ready to go again.

That's when Max pulled his right arm back and landed a clean punch to the cowboy's jaw. The disturbing sound of knuckle hitting bone filled the room. All the women seemed to gasp in horror. With his arms spinning like windmills, the Cowboy tumbled backward and crashed into the aquarium. The glass shattered with tropical fish pouring onto the floor alongside the unconscious cowboy.

I remember being worried about the fish and wanting to scoop them up in my skirt and put them in some water in the kitchen. But before I could, Max pulled me by the wrist out the front door. When we got outside Abel was standing on the lawn. "Dude, you totally knocked that guy out," he said.

"The fucking jerk grabbed Wendy's ass right in front of me," Max said, through tight lips.

I abhorred violence, but I loved the fact that Max had protected me. For the first time in my life I felt safe with someone. It was in that moment that Max became my savior, my hero and my guardian angel all rolled up in one. I pledged right there and then I would never let this guy get away.

Phone Home-1991

Privacy was non-existent in jail. During the day the noise could be deafening. Rock radio or oldies played over the PA system constantly. Television blared from the day room. Restless inmates milled around with voices so loud it hurt. There was nowhere to go to get a reprieve or find a slice of silence. As I laid in my bunk the grief and regret would come in waves. It was excruciating. Unbearable. I felt the same sadness and loneliness I felt when I was a kid. With nothing to anesthetize the repressed emotions, they started to percolate just under the surface.

I thought if I could call someone and hear a familiar, soothing voice it would make me feel better. But I was pretty damn sure there was no one in the free world who wanted to hear from me ever again. Furthermore, my home phone had been disconnected for a few months because I hadn't paid the bill. My dad wasn't around anymore because he had passed away from cirrhosis of the liver a long time ago. My sister, Diane, had cut me off ten years before because she couldn't stand watching me circle the drain. With my old friends who had all but disappeared, sadly, my life had been chiseled down to a cheating husband and a few sketchy tweakers.

As I laid there, I desperately wanted to talk to my boys. Then I remembered my next door neighbor, Patty. As the apartment manager, I had once done Patty a huge favor by renting her a one-bedroom even though she had really bad credit. Patty always said she was indebted to me, so I figured it was a good time to collect.

After morning chores passed inspection, the day officer flipped the switch to turn on the pay phones. I joined the other women who were waiting in line. When it was my turn, I punched in zero, followed by Patty's phone number which was one of the few numbers I knew by heart. A recording came on and asked for my name. There was a few more clicks until I heard: *"This call is originating from a Los Angeles County correctional facility. If you wish to accept a collect call please push number one."* Another click and Patty came on the line. "Wendy?"

"Thank you for taking my call."

"You alright girl?"

"I'm kicking pretty bad ..."

"What the hell happened the other night?"

"Max was fucking cheating on me."

"Well, Max is telling everyone that he wasn't cheating on you and you just lost your mind."

"He's a fucking liar," I said through clenched teeth. I wanted everyone to know just how badly I had been betrayed.

I could tell Patty was smoking as she let out a long exhale.

"You're damn lucky the bullet only hit her in the arm. It could have been a whole lot worse you know."

Of course I had thought about that over and over again. If the bullet had gone a few inches the other way, I might have been up against murder charges. If ever there was a case of seconds and inches this would have been it.

"How's she doing?" I asked.

"Oh, she's doing great considering Max moved her into your bed the same night you went to jail."

"No. Fucking. Way."

I couldn't believe it. It was beyond my compression. I pressed my forehead against the phone as a tornado of emotions were let loose inside me. I couldn't think straight. Rage, hurt and despair swirled inside my chest.

How could Max move someone into my bed before it's even had a chance to cool off.

"I, I, I can't believe he'd do that to me ..." I finally said.

"I'm afraid it's even worse. Cat's been wearing all your clothes."

"What? That fucking bitch!" The blood was swirling in my ears.

"Yup. It's scandalous."

"Where are the boys at right now?"

"I heard them playing in there earlier this morning."

"Could you please see if they can come to the phone?"

"Hold on lets me see if I can find them." When Patty set down the phone I heard the clicking of her shoes and the screen door slamming shut.

I thought about talking to Rikki and Jerry, but how the hell would I explain what had happened that night? I had no idea.

My ears perked up when I heard Rikki's voice. In my mind I could see his lanky frame and his Dodger's baseball cap pulled down over his eyes. He picked up the phone and said, "Hello?"

"Rikki is that you?"

"Where are you Mom?" His voice was stern.

"Hi. I'm … I'm in jail Rikki. But I'll be home just as soon as I get this whole mess straightened out."

I still thought there was a slim chance I might get out.

"Where's Jerry at?" I asked.

"He said, he doesn't want to talk to you."

I was crushed as I imagined Jerry never speaking to me again and no one could really blame him if he didn't.

Trying to salvage at least one relationship, I whispered into the phone. "I love you so much Rikki."

There was silence.

Then, Rikki said, "I dont know if I love you anymore, Mom."

His words felt like a hot knife plunged straight into my heart. It felt like everything would go black.

"But, Rikki, what … what do you mean?"

"Why did you try to shoot dad?"

It was obvious that Max had already told the boys his version of what had happened. Instead of answering in a truthful manner, I lied. "I, I, I didn't know the gun was loaded."

"If you didn't know it was loaded why did you shoot twice?"

At nine years old my son was obviously much smarter than his incarcerated mother.

"I'm so sorry Rikki. I'm really, really sorry…"

A recording clicked on: *This call will be disconnected in thirty seconds.*"

I gripped the receiver, "Please tell Jerry I love him and I'm sorry for everything…"

Another click and an empty hollow silence. It was hard to decipher if the hollowness was coming from the phone or coming from inside of me.

"Rikki? Rikki? Are you there?"

I don't remember hanging up the phone. I don't remember walking back to my bunk. I don't remember if I cried. But what I do remember is the excruciating pain of disappointing my children. I had one son who wouldn't talk to me and another whose words played over and over inside my brain. I don't know if I love you Mom. I don't know if I love you. I don't know if I love you Mom. I don't know if I love you.

My Day In Court

Friday became Monday and back to Friday again. Time had become nothing more than a meaningless abstraction. My whole body ached. My toes. My arms. And especially my heart. As I laid on the skinny mattress, I stared at the names scratched into the layers of green paint on the bunk above me. I was sweating and freezing as the built-up toxins seeped from my body. My flesh glistened with a thin layer of sweat. I could hear the sound of women's voices as they yelled inside the dorm. I wanted to scream at them, 'to shut the fuck up'. But, I knew better. Besides, I was consumed with the hateful voices inside my own damn head.

I'm a washed-up piece of shit. I'll never amount to anything. Just let me die right here in this jail. I'll never ask for anything again.

If it weren't for Susan taking me under her wing those early days, I don't know if I would have made it. She gave me a tooth-brush, toothpaste and soap. Once she even laid a whole pack of cigarettes on my bunk right next to me.

"You don't have to do that...." I could barely lift my head off the paper-machete pillow.

"Someone did it for me, so I'm just passing it on." When Susan smiled her whole face lit up.

"Are you feeling any better today?" she asked.

"Maybe a little." I sighed. "But what I wouldn't do for an aspirin."

"Why don't you go to the nurse's line?"

"Because I don't want to end up in the infirmary like I did eight years ago when I was kicking. If it wasn't for someone finding me flopping around on the floor like a fish and calling an ambulance I might have died up there."

"Holy shit! I've heard horror stories about the infirmary, but I didn't know if they were true."

"The stories are true alright. I even had one nurse tell me, 'you put it in you now you shit it out.'"

"What the hell were you kicking anyway?"

"Methadone and Valiums which makes heroin a walk in the park."

I knew Susan had kicked heroin before but she told me she never used methadone because she had heard plenty about the brutal kick. I, on the other hand, had heard about it, but didn't listen. Just like everything else in my life, I had to find out the hard way.

Susan continued to check in on me until eventually my scrambled meth-head brain started to sort itself out. With some of my cognition coming back on line, I started to think about my next court date. At my arraignment, the public defender told me that assault with a deadly weapon could carry up to seven years. I knew the legal system enough to know that public defender's would always give the defendant the worst-case scenario so you'd jump on any plea bargain they offered later on.

When the morning of my court appearance came, a sheriff tapped her flashlight on my bunk at four thirty a.m. In a firm voice she said, "You're on the docket for court this morning. You need to get up."

After getting dressed in my county blues I joined other women who were going to court. We were all given our street clothes to change into and afterward taken to men's central jail a few miles away. There were over fifty black and white LA County buses lined up in rows in a massive parking lot.

We were put into a holding tank to wait some more. Finally, they called my name and I was cuffed to the wrist of a girl who was going to the same court as me. We were escorted through a cloud of thick diesel exhaust to a bus that would take us all the way to court. As soon as we stepped on board we were blasted by obscenities from sex-starved-shackled men who were locked behind a thick mesh door.

"Yo baby, show us some tits," one of them yelled.

When I glanced in the back there was a greasy biker who licked the edges of his lips with his pointy tongue. I cringed. It made my skin crawl with disgust. Having to endure the men's disrespect when you already feel like a piece of shit, was the worst part of going to court.

The women were locked inside a tiny compartment. As we sat in silence with our shoulders pressed together, I could smell years of built up body odor and piss. I shifted, trying my best to get comfortable in the tight quarters. Finally there was a jerky, rumble underneath as the bus lurched forward to join a caravan. Dozens of black and white buses took off in the mornings for court houses all over Los Angeles.

As we drove, I gazed out the hazy window at the vast blue sky above. Its enormity ripped my mind right out of my small, incarcerated world. My eyes scanned all the people who were on their way to work or taking their kids to school. As I watched the cars and landscape whiz by it made me realize, once again, that nothing had stopped just because I was behind bars. Everything was going on in the world exactly as it had, with or without me. This realization made me feel insignificant. Like I was nothing more than a walking shell of a human being. My self-hatred owned me and I was convinced I would never get free from it.

About an hour passed before we were ushered into another holding tank at Torrance Superior Court. It had faded yellow walls, a pay phone and a shared open toilet in the corner. I sat down on the cold concrete bench and waiting in dread with my hair falling in my face. The "not knowing" was the absolute worst part of doing time. I thought at least if I was sentenced I could start crossing the days off my calendar. The minutes ticked by slowly, until finally, the door slid open and a crew-cut sporting Sheriff called my name. He escorted me to a small room where my state-appointed public defender waited in his wrinkled, unkempt suit. The Sheriff took off my handcuffs. I rubbed my wrists as I took a seat at the small table.

My attorney flipped through my thick file and I stared at the red capillaries crisscrossing his nose. I figured he was probably a bitter alcoholic just like my dad.

Finally, he looked up, his brow creased, and said, "The prosecutor has offered you two years in state penitentiary with a lid on it and three years of probation if you plead guilty today."

My heart sank. A 'lid on it' would mean I would serve every single day of the two years. I couldn't stand being away from Rikki and Jerry that long.

"I was thinking more like a year in the county jail," I countered.

He raised an eyebrow. "You want a year in the county jail?"

"No one is going to testify so the prosecution doesn't have a case," I shot back.

"How do you know?"

"A friend told me that my ex doesn't want to take the stand."

"But I just saw your husband *with his girlfriend* in the court-room," he said.

I felt like I was slipping in quicksand but I tried to appear calm.

"Can you talk to him? I'm sure he'll tell you he doesn't want to testify."

"You want me to talk to your husband?"

"You're representing me and I think that would be a good place to start." I stared him down.

He stood up and tucked the file under his arm. "I can talk to them but I doubt the prosecution will give you a year."

"Then we're going to trial." I shrugged.

I knew that the 'system' was looking to move cases through because they didn't want to tie-up the courts or use unnecessary tax payer's dollars. Threatening to take it to trial was the only leverage I had. I could see the contempt coming from behind my attorney's red-rimmed eyes. *Fucker*, I thought. *You don't care what happens to me.* He tapped on the back of the locked door and the bailiff let him into the hallway.

As I waited, my stomach did somersaults. I wanted a cigarette, a Valium, anything to take the edge off.

Later the Sheriff came back and led me handcuffed like an animal to its slaughter through brightly lit hallways. When I walked in the courtroom I immediately saw the two of them sitting in the front row. Cat looked away while Max slipped lower in his seat. A searing hot knife plunged into my heart as I walked towards the public defender. My fingers curled into tight fists, my nails dug into my palms. It felt like I was holding my breath under water.

The public defender leaned over and whispered in my ear. "Good news Wendy. They have agreed to give you a year in the county jail."

I couldn't even enjoy that small victory because I was reeling with emotions.

This can't be happening. Why is he doing this to me. Doesn't he love me anymore?

More than anything I felt the unfairness of it all. The inarguable injustice of someone who I had once loved beyond life itself was choosing to be with someone else. I was hurting so much it felt like I had taken a physical beating. My shoulders tensed up. There was an ever-present tightness behind my sternum.

The judge flipped through the pages of my lengthy rap sheet while he sat on his elevated platform behind his massive desk. Although he was just a few feet from me, he seemed far away. It felt like everything was blurred and indistinct. Intensely real and unreal at the same time. All of it spiraling. I felt on the verge of panic but tried my best not to show it. Act normal, I told myself.

"Wendy Mendias?" The judge snapped me back into the moment.

"Yes, your honor."

"You are being charged with assault with a deadly weapon. How do you plead?"

"Guilty, your honor."

My mouth moved and I was able to form the needed words but my mind was black with rage. How could Max sit in the courtroom with another woman while the guillotine came down on his wife's neck? How could he just throw away all our history together for a twenty-four-year-old tweaker? My face was growing hot. Enraged, I wanted to tell the judge, the courtroom and anyone who would listen how badly my husband had betrayed me. I wanted to scream, jump over the divider, pummel Max with my fists and claw out her eyes. I wanted blood.

But I didn't do any of that. Instead I contained the cauldron boiling inside of me. But that kind of rage has to go somewhere. I stored mine inside the vault with all the other failures and disappointments of my life.

The judge recited legal jargon, using words like stipulation, due process, a speedy trial and blah, blah, blah. "I hereby sentence you to one year in the county jail with credit for time served."

This meant I would miss my kids' entire summer. I would miss Thanksgiving. I would miss Christmas. I would miss their birthdays and wouldn't get out until after New Years. My chest heaved with despair. I pushed back the tears that threatened to fill my eyes. My feet shifted back and forth. I wanted to run. I wanted to hide. I wanted to die.

When the judge finished his speech, he snapped the file closed and the sheriff escorted me out of the courtroom. As I passed by Max I lacerated him with my eyes. I may have looked like a bad ass on the outside but what no one knew was I was starting to crack.

Parenthood (1975)

Back when I was twenty-two I prided myself as someone who could use heroin in moderation. That is, until I found myself shivering and throwing up first thing in the morning. It had been six months of using every day and I was hooked. But it all came to a screeching halt when I found out I was pregnant. This was a conundrum of epic proportion. I wasn't ready to have children, but Max surprised me when he said, "This could be a blessing in disguise."

"Are you kidding? We're strung out like dogs. Don't you think I should get an abortion?"

"If we had a baby it would motivate us to stay clean."

Although I wasn't ready to have children I was a co-dependent through and through. So, if Max wanted a baby, I would give him one. But first, I insisted we'd have to get clean.

In the mid-seventies, Camarillo State Mental Hospital was the only option for a medical detox and it was free. I knew the facility well. Not only had I been there when I cut my wrists but, my mother had been there many times when she had her psychotic breaks.

The next day I called them to get on the waiting list, which could often take weeks before a bed opened up. But when I told them I was pregnant I got pushed to the top of the list and within days Max and I got beds. Camarillo Hospital was nestled in between rolling grassy hills and a patchwork of vegetable farms an hour outside of Los Angeles.

The actual detox unit was as long as a football field. Max would be in the men's dorms and I would be in the women's. The day room was a common area where everyone could hang out, smoke cigarettes, and watch television. Junkies, pill heads, and alcoholics came from all over Los Angeles, Ventura, and Riverside to clean up. While the alcoholics were usually detoxed with sedatives, a dope fiend could expect a 21-day methadone tapper. The first days weren't so bad, but as they dropped the milligrams, my symptoms got worse. My bones and muscles ached. I couldn't sleep. It felt like I had lead in my calves. By my second week I was complaining to the nurses.

"I'm not feeling the medication anymore."

"That's probably because we're lowering your dose."

"I think you're taking me down too fast."

"Tell your counselor you're not satisfied with the dosage protocol maybe she could help you."

Debbie had short black hair, piercing blue eyes and an edge that came from all the years of being a drug addict herself. Sitting across from my counselor in the cubbyhole office, I stated my case.

"I think they are taking me off the methadone too fast."

An eyebrow curled up. "Here's what I'm thinking. You need to go to the ninety-day program," she said. "A twenty-one day detox isn't long enough to get strong."

"What?" That was not the answer I was looking for.

"You need to address why you need drugs to function in life."

"But Max has a job when we get out, and I'm going to…"

Interrupting me, she said, "You think Max having a job will keep you from doing drugs?"

"No but having a baby will."

"That's even more reason why you need to get a solid foundation."

While ninety days sounded way too long, I believed Debbie. I had been doing drugs or alcohol pretty much since my early teens and didn't know how to stop. There was something fundamentally wrong with me. Maybe it was time to see if a therapist could help me figure out what it was. Besides, we had nowhere to live and while Max's brother promised him a job, it would still be there after we did the program.

A few days later, while Max and I sat in the dayroom, I started to press him. "We need to take this opportunity to get clean," I said.

Max narrowed his eyes. "What does that mean?"

"This might be our only chance and I don't want to screw it up. We need to go into the 90 day program."

Eventually, Max agreed and after three weeks of detoxing we went to the 90 day where we would start working on ourselves. When we entered the dorm it looked like a freak show. Some patients wore cardboard signs around their necks with statements like, 'I AM A LIAR' or 'I HAVE A POTTY MOUTH.' Everyone carried a yellow legal pad and we were expected to write our life stories down.

The program was based on the Synanon model, a drug treatment center for junkies in the fifties and sixties. It was a hardcore philosophy that insisted addicts give up all their earthly possessions and surrender to the self-contained life style of the program. While it was eventually shut down for tax evasion and a corrupt leader, some of its philosophy carried over to other treatment centers. Part of that was a group therapy called The Game. This was where someone was put on a hot seat and made to endure harsh criticism (often yelling) from their peers. For instance, if I saw someone not doing their chores correctly, I was supposed to call them out on it. We were told that this form of attack therapy would break down the addict's inflated ego, which was needed to stay clean. While the whole 'in your face' approach was scary to me, I was lucky because no one wanted to yell at a pregnant woman.

Even in this crazy situation, I still had a lot of feelings come up. Maybe because I was clean or maybe because I was in the same institution as my mother, memories of her started to surface. One day sitting in meditation I had a flash back of being a small child carried by a fireman onto the front lawn. In my mind's eye I saw a snap shot of my mother: wild-eyed, strapped down on a gurney, being loaded into an ambulance. What I remember mostly was the seething shame I felt as neighbors stared from their windows at us. At six-years-old I knew my mother's insanity was supposed to be a secret, but now everyone in my neighborhood had found out.

It would be years later when I would learn that my mother had turned on the gas in the house after Dad stormed off to the local bar. While it's obvious she wanted to die, I was tortured by the fact that my mother would have killed us all to get her way. This was way too hard to come to terms with back then. Now I knew, I had to do whatever it would take not to make the same mistakes with my kids.

While in there I started seeing a local obstetrician. Eight weeks later my stomach popped out like I'd swallowed a basketball. It was very sweet how everyone took care of me. If I had a craving for something someone would find a way to get it for me. If I was cold, I would be handed a blanket. I had never been so pampered before and I loved the attention I was getting from my peers.

I started to daydream about Max and I and our new baby living in our own place. I imagined Max working while I stayed home and cooked dinner for him every night.

Meanwhile, during our free time at Camarillo Hospital, Max and I would sit in the dayroom and talk about our baby's name.

"If it's a girl I want to name her Brianna," I said.

"I like Jerry for a boy." Max's brown eyes had turned crystal clear and our relationship was so much better when we weren't on drugs.

* * *

One day when I had come full term, I remember lying down when a pain shot straight through me. I was in fucking labor. When I moaned someone brought a cool washcloth for my forehead. Another girl kept reminding me to breathe deep. Max stood in the threshold since he wasn't allowed to come into our dorm.

My breathing turned ragged. Every muscle in my body cramped. Sweat beaded on my face. Why hadn't anyone told me childbirth was so hard? It was times like these I missed having a mother the most. That powerful and primal longing bubbled up in me when I least expected it. I wanted a mother (or at least my idea of what one should look like) standing beside me whispering words of encouragement to get me through the horrific ordeal.

Finally, I was taken in an ambulance to St John's hospital and checked into the maternity ward. Soon there was a pretty blond nurse in blue scrubs checking to see how far along I was.

"You're only three centimeters," she said, looking up from between my legs.

"What does that mean?"

"You're not ready."

I hadn't had any education or read any books on giving birth so, I was completely in the dark.

Minutes later she was shaving my pubic hair and belly, which seemed strange. "Why are you shaving my stomach?" I asked.

"In case you need a cesarean."

At twenty-two I was unprepared for all of it, including the enema so you didn't lose control on the delivery table.

I remember Max's face was flushed when he got there. "You okay?" His brow creased like a paper fan.

"It really hurts."

He tenderly pushed a strand of my hair away from my face. He looked at me with love in his big brown eyes. Then another contraction hit and my whole face scrunched up. Every time a wave of pain came I squeezed Max's hand. I threw up in a bed pan. After twenty-four hours of contractions, my doctor finally arrived.

"Your still not dilating so we're going to need to do a caesarian," he said. At that point they could have turned me upside down and shaken the baby out of me if it would have stopped the fucking pain.

Moments later I was rushed on a gurney by hospital technicians to the operating room. Under bright fluorescent lights, I was placed on a table where my belly was opened up like a piece of fruit. Then the most beautiful thing happened. My son was brought into the world and gasped his first breath. All the hours of agony disappeared in an instant. I was filled with awe and such wonder that this beautiful, perfect creature came from inside of me. Before I even had a chance to hold my baby, the doctor knocked me out with Demerol.

When I woke up hours later, Max was standing at my side with a single red rose in his hand. "Thank you for giving me a baby boy. It's what I've always wanted."

Everything was finally going to be all right. Max and I were both clean. I had just given birth to a perfectly healthy child. I was determined to do things differently than my parents had. When I got to hold Jerry for the first time I felt a love like I had never felt before. It was so pure, so raw and so real. I studied his tiny fingers, little toes and his oval face. He was absolute perfection. My heart overflowed with love for this beautiful baby boy. For the first time at twenty-two, I was filled with possibilities of doing something worthwhile with my life. I was Jerry's mother. I would give him everything I never had growing up. But first I'd have to finish the drug program and by then, I only had weeks to go.

My mother-in-law came to the hospital room with a diaper bag hanging over her shoulder. Her long salt and pepper hair framed her weathered skin. It was from years of gardening in the hot sun, but whenever she smiled it took nearly ten years off of her life.

"Such a beautiful baby," Jennie said, holding a hand over her heart.

"We named him Jerry," I smiled.

"That's a perfect name. Don't worry, Wendy, I'll take care of him until you and Max get back on your feet."

It was hard letting him go but, it felt like I had no choice. I smelt the baby freshness of his scalp and kissed him on his soft forehead. "Goodbye Little Jerry. Mommy will see you soon." I handed him over, wrapped inside a receiving blanket like a burrito. Jennie cradled him in the crook of her arm. I told myself over and over I was doing the right thing. I had to be strong in order to stay sober.

However, when I went back to Camarillo Hospital I couldn't stop sobbing. I was a wreck. It felt like I was engulfed in a dark cloud. I was so depressed and had no idea why. I know now that it wasn't normal for a mother to be separated from her child like that. My heart was longing to hold Jerry in my arms and give him the love I never had. But I missed that opportunity. And unfortunately, I would miss so much more.

After we completed the program, Max and I were encouraged to get jobs within the hospital to gain employment skills and save money to get our own place. While we were in a hurry, we had nowhere to go so we moved into the homes behind the hospital which were dilapidated, two-story buildings with single rooms, a sink and a shared bathroom in the hall.

Back in those days most drug rehabs didn't promote complete abstinence. So we were allowed to drink alcohol, just as long as we didn't do any hard drugs. On Friday and Saturday nights all of the alumni of the ninety day program would gather in a room and start pounding down wine or beer. There would be so many of us sometimes there would be standing room only.

One of my friends, Ann, who I knew from Santa Monica went through the program after me. She was single and shy, so I always made sure she was included with any soirée that was happening on the employee grounds.

One night we were all drinking and laughing while Led Zeppelin played from a tinny radio. Then Max got so buzzed he ruined it all, teasing me about a dinner I cooked the week before.

"You guys should taste Wendy's beef stew," he laughed.

"Why? Is it good?" One of the guys asked.

"The gravy was a little thick. A fork could stand straight up in it."

I scowled because he was embarrassing me.

To make matters worse he started singing a sixties song by the Association using his own lyrics, "Who's walking down the streets of the city, who makes a stew that's lighter than air. Everyone knows it's Wendy. And Wendy has stormy eyes...."

"Shut the fuck up Max," I slugged him on the arm.

"Who's cooking up a pasty stew in the kitchen, everyone knows its Wendy."

Everyone laughed and Max wouldn't let up on his singing. I was furious and stormed out of the room, slamming the door behind me. I stomped back to our room. I was sure Max would follow me and apologize for embarrassing me. But as the minutes ticked by he never came. An hour later there was still no sign of him. That pissed me off even more. How dare him, I thought.

When I walked back to the party to see why he hadn't come everyone was gone. Where the hell was Max? I went to Ann's room to see if she knew. I knocked on her door. Silence. I knocked harder. I heard a soft rustle of sheets. Someone was in there so why weren't they answering the door? A tightness squeezed around my throat. Then it hit me. Max is in there with her. I clenched my fists as I kicked in the door. The shoddy construction gave way. Max was sitting on the mattress with Ann who had a sheet up to her chin to hide her naked body. Little did I know that years later this would happen again.

"You fucking bitch." I lunged forward. I went for her throat. Wrapping my fingers around it I squeezed. My face was hot. My brain on fire. Spit was spewing from my mouth as I called her names. All of the sudden Max grabbed me from behind with both arms in a bear hug. Sweaty, he lifted me up and carried me with legs kicking in the air. "You mother fucker! How could you do this to me?" I screamed.

"Please Wendy let me explain." He set me down in the hallway. I stepped back. My chest was heaving. My breathing jagged.

"How could you do this?"

"It's not what it looks like." His upheld palms extended.

"I fucking loved you!"

"Let me explain, baby."

Why is it men always want to explain after they get caught in the act? What's to explain? 'I'm sorry honey but my dick accidently went into her vagina when I wasn't paying attention.' My molars grinded inside my mouth. My eyes narrowed into slits.

"How could you, you-you fucking asshole?"

I ran back to our room. Rage burned inside my brain. That night I told Max to get out. He moved to Los Angeles to stay with his Mom and our baby. I was so damn clueless back then I thought these kind of things never happened, especially with one of your best friends.

As the weeks passed, Max kept calling and begging for my forgiveness. I was angry but would listen to his apologies anyway. I didn't know anything else but him and the need for a family caused me to ignore all the obvious red flags. Two months later he had saved enough money from his new job to get a small guest house. I joined him there and without any support we would end up using drugs again. This went on until eight years later I found myself pregnant again. By then I had all but forgotten Max's first betrayal. And as soon as Rikki was born I fell madly and deeply in love. Again. But sadly, not even the love of my children could keep me from doing drugs.

Divorce; The Jail House Way

The day after court I leaned over the bathroom sink tugging on my wedding band with a fierce determination to pry it off. If I would have had a knife I might have chopped the entire finger off at the bone.

Ever since the night I went to jail, I had been searching my memory banks for that one thing that would help me understand just how my marriage had fallen apart. While it might have been obvious that drugs had played a big part, I couldn't see that yet because everything in me was still blaming Cat for breaking up my so called "happy home."

Susan was standing beside me with her thick hair pulled back in a pony tail. "Maybe if you pull and twist at the same time?" she said.

"I did, but there's a thick pad of skin underneath and it won't come off." I sighed.

Susan pulled out a plastic bottle of baby oil from her ditty bag that she had draped over her shoulder like a purse. "This will help."

"I doubt it. It's on there pretty damn tight."

Squirting the clear oily substance around the gold braided band, she gently twisted it in a circular motion.

"I'm telling you, it won't budge." I said that just as the ring slipped off and pinged across the tiled floor.

"Oh my God you did it!" I rushed over to pick it up.

Susan puffed out her chest with pride. "Just needed my special touch was all."

"You are such the shit girlfriend."

"So now what are you up to?" Susan asked.

"I'm going to see what I can get for it."

"But it's your wedding band."

"Look, he came to court *with her*," I nearly spat out the words. "That would seem like an indication that our marriage is over don't you think. Besides, I want to buy some cigarettes."

"I'll give you cigarettes if that's all you need...."

"You've done way too much already." I held up my hand refusing her offer. "I'm going to see if Smiley wants it."

Everyone in the dorm knew that Smiley, a cute Hispanic stud broad ran the dorm's store. She was known for selling candy and cigarettes. As an entrepreneur she'd stock up and when everyone ran out of goodies she'd sell her shit for double the price. I figured since she was a good business woman, she'd be interested in buying the ring.

Smiley was reclined on her bunk with a young girl chatting her up. As I approached I held back a moment until Smiley, looked up with her long coal black hair draping her face and noticed me. "Can I help you?" The girl sensing business was afoot, excused herself.

I stepped closer holding the ring in my palm. "I thought you might be interested in this?"

Smiley's nickname obviously came from her perfect Chicklets teeth that she flashed when she plucked the ring from my hand. With a furrowed brow she held it up to the light to examine how many karats it might be. I looked around to make sure no one was watching. I was embarrassed by my desperation but, not enough to let it stop me.

"Why are you're selling your wedding band?"

"Because I'm not with him anymore." I bit down on my lower lip. Just saying it out loud made it more real.

Smiley nodded. "I'll give you thirty bucks for it."

"Oh, come on, it's worth much more than that ..."

"Look, if you're not interested..." Smiley's voice trailed off.

"But it's real gold."

"And this is *real* jail baby. You aren't going to get any more for it in here." Her tone sounded almost sympathetic.

"How about giving me fifty bucks?"

"Thirty-five. And that's the best I can do."

Susan stood down the aisle shaking her head no. But I was determined and turned my head back towards Smiley. "Will you throw in a pack of cigarettes?"

"Sure, why not?"

Reaching into her over-stuffed ditty bag Smiley's hand disappeared inside. Her brown eyes darted back and forth until she brought out a pack of Marlboros and slapped them into my hand. After that she pulled out a wad of cash from her bra and peeled off some sweaty bills.

"Thanks Smiley." I turned to leave.

A few minutes later I sat on my thin mattress, with my back against the wall, puffing away. But sadly, not even the cigarettes and a bit of cash could stop the white noise inside my brain. As the gray smoke swirled, I kept seeing Max and Cat sitting in that courtroom together behind my mind's eye. And although I had experienced a lot of loss in my life, this felt like someone had plunged a knife straight into my heart and left it there. The searing pain made me want to curl up in the fetal position and sob into a puddle of tears. But lord knows I couldn't do that because my survival greatly depended on me pretending like I was a badass woman who was used to doing time.

The Truth

It had been nearly two months at Sybil Brand. I was still weak but, getting a bit stronger every day. At times it felt like the bone-crushing depression would take me down. I had to keep chanting to myself not to cry. I felt like road kill that only kept moving because my heart didn't know enough to stop pumping blood.

Losing Max was like a death to me. Only worse because he was still alive. How was it one day we were together as man and wife, and the next day I was locked up and he was with someone else? With plenty of time to think I traced and retraced much of our history together. But that didn't help much. When I slept I had strange dreams that would cause me to bolt straight up in my bunk, drenched in sweat. I'd have to look around to get my bearings. Then I'd remember, oh yeah, I'm locked up and my husband is sleeping with someone else. I imagined myself dying a thousand deaths. Of hanging myself in a shower stall. Of throwing myself over the ramp on the way to the chow-hall.

If I could just shift everything into reverse and go back to that night I would do it all differently. If I were to get a do-over when Cat showed up at the door I would tell her, 'no go away. It's too late to get more speed.' Or better yet, how about I never bought that stupid gun in the first place. I played out scenarios over and over in my head. I knew I couldn't change the past but it didn't stop me from ruminating about it.

A few days later when I called Patty again she had more bad news.

"Max is selling all your things."

My breath caught in my throat. "What do you mean?"

"He got evicted and he is trying to get rid of everything."

"But he can't do that, those are my things…"

"Well yeah, I don't think he really cares at this point..."

"If they're evicted where are they going to go?" I gripped the receiver in my hand so hard it's a wonder it wasn't crushed.

"I have no idea."

After I hung up my thoughts spun in a whirlpool of sad and angry and frightened and pointless. I knew I had to do something. Anything to help Jerry and Rikki. But what? I couldn't protect my children from behind bars. I was completely powerless. Then a strange voice of reason inside my head told me to call Jennie for help. But my next thought was, *I'm sure your mother-in-law doesn't want to hear from you. Don't burden her with all your problems again. She has to be sick of your bullshit and who could blame her if she was.*

I didn't eat much for the next few days. I couldn't swallow over the perpetual lump in my throat. The worry seized me. Gripped me from on the inside. I couldn't take it. I had to do something and Jennie was my only option.

Desperate, when it was my turn at the phone I punched in her phone number. I thought for sure she'd refuse my collect call as I held the receiver close to my ear.

"Hello?" Her voice sounded cold.

"Thank you so much for accepting my call Jennie. I just, I really needed to talk to you..."

"Hi Wendy. What do you want to talk about?"

"I'm actually calling about the boys. I'm worried about them."

There was a pause. "Why is that?"

"Max is doing methamphetamine. Actually, we both were doing it."

"You guys were doing it around the kids?"

"Well, no. I mean, they never saw us or anything ... we always made sure they weren't around."

Saying that out loud made me realize just how ridiculous I sounded. We all lived under the same roof for fucks sake. We were horrible parents. "Yeah, I guess we were doing it around the kids."

I laid out my lengthy confession to Jennie, telling her everything. Hell, it was the most honest I had been in I don't know how long. And I wasn't doing it because I was suddenly struck with high morals. I was doing it because I was desperate and Jennie was the only one who could help. After I finished talking I waited for a response but Jennie was silent as the music played from the PA system overhead. I shifted nervously back and forth afraid of what might be coming next.

"I'm going to get to the bottom of this and find out what's going on," Jennie said.

"Thank you, Jennie. Please find out what's going on." Jennie loved my boys and I knew she'd do whatever it took to intervene on their behalf.

"Just get your shit together Wendy."

"I want to. I really do." I said those words never believing I actually could.

When I called the following week Rikki was there. Jennie didn't say anything about Max but she told me the plan was for Rikki to live there until the day I got out, while Jerry would stay with his friend so he could finish high school. Just knowing my boys were safe made me feel relieved.

Parenting Class

It was around six weeks into my sentence when I was lying on my bunk and heard over the PA system, "Adamson, line it up for parenting class."

"Shit! Fuck!" I hit my head on the top bunk when I got up too fast.

For Christ sake! Can't a girl get some privacy around here? Does everyone in the dorm need to know my frigging business?

I slipped into the hard-plastic sandals and shuffled to the front, where surprise, more bad moms were lining up to go to class. I felt a sharp tug of humiliation at the base of my neck. I shoved my hands deep into the pockets and studied the swirls of wax on the recently buffed floor. Parenting class was a stipulation rattled off by the judge the day I had gone to court. I blamed Max for the inconvenience. That was how my brain was wired. If he hadn't been cheating on me I wouldn't have used the gun and wouldn't have to attend those dreaded classes in the first place.

The lock released with a hollow thud and an officer yelled, "Line it up against the wall ladies."

The corridor was sometimes like a wind tunnel with air sweeping through. Goose bumps formed on my flesh. I fell into the back of the line standing as erect as a soldier in the military.

"Let's move it ladies." The officer said, keys bouncing off her thick hip.

When we came to the end of the hall we were led into an enclosed courtyard surrounded by tall cinderblock walls with razor wire that looped along the top. The cool evening air slapped me in my face. A sliver of moon hung in the sky like a devious smile. I breathed in the night air like cocaine. It was laced with traces of freedom and just being out there made me miss Rikki and Jerry even more.

The L-shaped dilapidated prison school building needed a paint job. We were escorted to a brightly lit room that had rows of metal fold-out chairs already set up. An old projector was locked and loaded with a shaft of light directed towards the wall. The women filed in and when I sat down the cold metal seat sent shivers up my spine. I was dreading the next hour and a half of class and wanted to be back in the dorm where I could relax on my bunk.

The officer stood alongside the projector. "Sorry, the popcorn machine is broken tonight ladies." Amused with herself, she laughed as she hit the switch.

The projector hummed as it threaded celluloid film through a metal box. The wall flickered with numbers: 10, 9, 8, 7, 6 … until the voice of the narrator introduced several families. I was riveted as the three mothers, the fathers, and all their children, who were going through divorce were being interviewed. All the adults were angry, the children confused as the intrusive camera followed them throughout their day. It felt like one of those documentaries where you watch the behaviors of gorillas in their natural habitat. We were voyeurs into these families lives. Where I would usually be easily distracted, I found myself paying attention.

One thin-lipped mother with blue eye-shadow gave orders to her teenage daughter to get the alimony check from her father during their weekly visit. Mom looked directly at the camera and said, "He won't listen to me so, maybe he'll listen to his own daughter." The pretty girl lowered her head seemingly embarrassed.

The film cuts to the father who had a receding hairline, a beer belly and was sitting on an oversized couch. "My Ex is just looking to get all my money." He shook his head in disgust.

Cut to a black mom by the name of Grace who also had a nine-year-old son. She was clearly pissed off at her husband and rightly so in my mind. "I caught him screwing around with another woman so I filed for divorce," she said.

Oh geez. There's another way to handle a cheating husband? Who knew?

It felt like watching a multi-collision-pile-up of broken souls and I couldn't look away. It was reality TV on steroids. Heated arguments, families having to move, kids having to start new schools. It was ugly. It was brutal. But more than anything it reminded me of the fights Max and I had towards the end. As I thought back on those times my foot started to tap uncontrollably. I cracked my knuckles one by one. It was like the universe was holding up a mirror so I could see myself and who I had become.

But I was shocked that these people had agreed to be documented on film during obviously, the worst time of their lives. I was brought up to keep all family business behind closed doors. We didn't talk to each other let alone someone else.

After watching the first segment, the film leaped forward five years and everyone got interviewed again. Sadly, not much had changed. It seemed as if they were stuck in some twisted time warp. The blue eye-shadowed mom was still trying to get money from the dead beat dad. The kids were now teenagers, some of them had started doing drugs and some were falling behind in school.

But when they interviewed Grace she somehow looked different. Younger even. Her clear brown eyes stared directly into the camera as she talked, "When we first met I was extremely depressed. I would sleep all day until I couldn't even take care of my son. Finally, my best friend who had some concerns about my well being insisted I get some help. For some reason, I listened to her and made an appointment with my old pastor who I hadn't seen for years. When we sat in his office I told him everything but, mostly I complained about what he had done to me. He just listened to me rant and rave and complain. When I finished he said, 'You need to pray for your ex-husband.' What? Pray for my ex? I thought that was a really stupid idea. Why did I have to pray for him when He was the one cheating on me."

Grace continued her story, "My Pastor asked me if I was tired of being angry and I told him yes, I was really, really tired of being mad all the time. He then gave me a prayer to say every day, '*Thank you God for giving my son the best father that he can be.*' Believe me I thought it was absurd, but I did it anyway. A couple weeks later I realized I wasn't being consumed by the usual rage. That prayer worked for me. I even went back to church where I met someone and fell in love again."

I related to Grace. I was tired of being angry. I was tired of living a life balled up into a tight fist. Grace had planted a seed and that's exactly what I needed at the time. I wondered if the prayer could work for me? I was in such pain it was certainly worth a try. Later that night while lying in my bunk, I said, *Thank you, for giving my children the best father that he can be.*

I didn't believe the words at all but, I said them anyway. In fact, I would say that prayer for weeks all throughout the day. Whenever my thoughts got snagged with resentment or revenge I'd chant that prayer inside my head.

Several weeks later, just like Grace, I felt a shift. It may not have been a massive one, but it came in the form of a clear succinct voice inside my head: You know, *Wendy, the best way to pay Max back would be to become a success.* But what does 'success' even look like, I wondered. Would it mean finding new man? Having a lot of money in the bank? Would it mean making amends to my boys? I didn't have a clue, one thing for certain, I'd have to be clean and sober to find out. And for the first time that became my goal.

The Smoking Ban

A few months into my sentence I was starting to get into a groove when it was announced by jail officials that on July 1st tobacco would no longer be allowed in any county facility. They were taking away our cigarettes. It seemed a cruel and unjust punishment and the very thing that could push us all over the edge.

The jailhouse canteen went from selling ten packs of cigarettes, to five, until they stopped carrying them altogether. A sense of panic spread throughout the jail. The ban was all anybody talked about and we blamed the Surgeon General for giving second-hand smoke such a bad rap.

It was insanely noisy and voices screeched in an effort to be heard. Tinny music was constantly pumped in through the PA system and there was always some drama going on. But with the threat of our last vice being taken from us there was a free-floating anxiety that hung densely in the air.

When the day arrived, an inmate yelled from the front of the dorm, "They're coming down the hall to get our cigarettes. Smoke 'em if you got 'em."

Susan and I were looking at magazines on my bunk when we heard the warning. We both lit-up taking a desperate drag of what may have been our last cigarette.

"I can't believe they're actually going to do this to us." Susan blew a puff of smoke.

"I thought maybe a judge would order an injunction to stop it."

A few minutes later, Officer Harris, a thick, beefy officer came stomping through the door with her male counterpart who dragged a green garbage bin with CONTRABAND written on the side.

Harris cupped her hands around her mouth, "Okay ladies, it's time to give up those cigarettes."

Women cursed, some slammed locker doors while others shot daggers with their eyes. In a pointless gesture of defiance everyone lit up at the same time. Within seconds a cloud of second-hand smoke formed above our heads.

Shelly, a black girl with braids who was obviously off her psych meds, started chanting, "Smoking is our constitutional right!" while circling the aisle like a nervous terrier. There was a standoff for a minute until one emaciated white girl with braids and a streetwalker's edge walked down the center aisle, blowing puffs of smoke all along the way. Harris glared at her as she crumbled up an empty pack of cigarettes and slammed dunked it into the contraband bin. When she turned around her long braids spun so fast they could have easily taken someone's eye out.

They obviously didn't want a riot so they gave us time to vent. But after our tantrums were over they took the bin to the next dorm while leaving behind a chorus of complaints in their wake. Everyone was agitated and by afternoon I wanted to tear my flesh right off the bone. My foot wouldn't stop tapping. Sweat beaded up on my forehead. My palms became clammy and cold.

The next day I took to pacing back and forth in the dorm. It didn't help. Nothing helped. Without nicotine everyone had hair-triggered mood swings. Arguments would break out for the silliest things. But two weeks into the ban I was inching towards my own version of acceptance. I figured if I had to quit in jail I'd just smoke an entire carton when I got out. I was lying on my bunk trying to focus on reading a book. When I glanced up I saw Susan rushing down the aisle with her ponytail swinging to and fro. She sat down on the edge of my bunk, "Guess what I got," she said, with a mischievous grin.

"What?" I sat up.

Susan craned her neck both ways before reaching inside her bra and pulling out a crumpled-up paper-towel. I scooted closer as she peeled back the corners to reveal a clump of loose tobacco in the center.

"Where the hell did you get that?"

"Chewie."

Susan was a trustee in admissions and had told me that Chewie was an industrial sized garbage disposal, six feet long with high, stainless steel walls and a conveyer belt that pushed everything towards blades where it would ultimately be pulverized.

"But how…?"

"A cop discarded a pack of Marlboros into Chewie and when she got called out of the room, I grabbed it before it got chopped to bits."

"I'm impressed." I shook my head as I tried to imagine it.

"The tobacco got a little wet so I emptied it into a paper towel."

"We can use the hair blower to dry it out."

It was late morning and most inmates were still at work so we headed to the bathroom. A lot of times there wouldn't even be an officer in their station and we were in luck. I pushed the round button to the blower, holding the tobacco in my hand under a stream of hot air. Susan stood behind me with an eye peeled for any intruders. The heat burned my hand but I would have crawled through shards of broken glass to have me a bit of nicotine.

When it was dry I grabbed a roll of toilet paper from above the sink. Susan and I headed back to my bunk where we tore the outer tissue into small squares that we could use as rolling papers.

"You may not believe this but, I never learned how to roll a joint," I confessed.

"No worries. I'm an old pro." Susan winked.

Pinching a bit of tobacco, Susan placed it into the fold of the paper. Pressing it between her two thumbs and index fingers, she rolled back and forth until it was the size of a knitting needle. When it was packed tight enough she wet the edge of the paper with the tip of her tongue and pressed it together. With a smile, she said. "How about the showers?"

"Good idea." We both stood up and rushed down the aisle.

Vinyl curtains with black mold running along the bottom edge gave privacy to six shower stalls. Susan and I slipped into the last one and stood nose to nose. Even though my heart was pounding with adrenaline, we couldn't help but laugh. It felt the same way when I snuck cigarettes in the bathroom back in junior high school. Susan then struck a contraband match and took the first hit. The red cherry flickered as sparks fell like fireworks towards our feet.

"Don't let the smoke go out," I waved my hand above her head.

When it came my turn I could feel the heat on my lips as I took that first hit. The harsh smoke burned the back of my throat. I held it in a moment to savor it. I became dizzy. It was the closest I had been to having a buzz, and as a true addict, I immediately wanted more.

Susan started getting it a lot after that. She was so good at snatching the contraband from Chewie we couldn't smoke it fast enough. So, being resourceful addicts and all, we decided to go into the tobacco slinging business together. It was merely a matter of supply and demand. The women would pay three to five bucks for a skinny rollie. While up until then I had been keeping a low profile, I was willing to take the risk to have my own pocket money.

I always loved the thrill of getting away with something illegal. But it didn't take long before we got lazy and instead of going to the showers to smoke we'd squat down by the side of my bunk. We figured since my bunk was all the way in the back and other inmates who saw us would follow the jailhouse code of silence and mind their own business. All except Crazy Shelly that is, who came over to us one day and asked, "Ya all think I can have shorts on that?" She stood at the end of the bunk with a smile.

I knew if I said no, Shelly might snitch on us, so, I handed her what was left of the roach. My eyes narrowed as I watched her wrap her full lips around the end sucking until the red cherry burned clear down to her fingertips.

From then on Shelly came over to ask for shorts every time we lit up. This went on for several weeks until I got tired of what I considered to be covert blackmail.

Susan and I decided to put a stop to it and when Shelly came over again, I told her, "You have to pay like everyone else."

"But I don't have any money and, and ..."

I held up my hand. "I'm sorry but no."

Shelly drew her lips tight before storming off. Shortly after, Susan and I decided to hide everything in case Shelly snitched. Good thing we did because the next day while Susan was at work in admissions, Officer Jenkins, with her jaw pulled tight, came strutting down the aisle.

"Where is your property?" Jenkins asked.

I silently pointed to the property box I stored under my bunk.

"Follow me." She grabbed the box.

I slipped my feet into my plastic sandals and walked behind her. A male officer was holding the door open for us. Once in the corridor I assumed the usual position with my back against the wall. Jenkins dropped the property box by my feet with a thud and got so close I could smell her coffee breath when she talked.

"I hear you're selling cigarettes in the dorm."

"No, officer," I lied.

"Well I'm going to have to search your property."

"Yes ma'am."

The male officer, sporting a crew cut, hovered with a thumb hooked in his belt as Jenkins riffled through my belongings. She opened my shampoo and with one eye glared inside. She shuffled through my papers and magazines. I nervously shifted back and forth while clasping both hands together to keep them from shaking. I knew crazy Shelly had snitched and I wanted revenge.

When Jenkins didn't find anything in my property she gave me a stern warning. "I'm going to be watching you from here on out. Do you hear me?"

"Yes ma'am." I nodded.

I was let back into the dorm and while I may have wanted revenge, I knew it was pointless because Shelly would only snitch on me again. Fortunately, the problem resolved itself when she was transferred that night to another dorm. And not until later, when I climbed into my bunk, would I realize that I was being a hypocrite. As I stared at the cinder block wall it occurred to me, if I had been busted for tobacco, I could have gotten more time added on to my sentence. If I wanted to see Rikki and Jerry again like I claimed, I needed to stop taking risks. I made a decision that I wouldn't smoke again until I got out.

Sugar Addict

As a kid I remember candy being used often as a bribe or enticement by the adults in my life. Every Easter, Halloween, Christmas we'd be given marshmallow bunnies and chocolate Santa's until we were sick to our stomachs. And later as a teen, I'd be sneaking off with half gallons of ice cream or Oreo cookies into my room. Sugar soothed me on some level and I was looking for relief.

It's no wonder that every cell in my body wanted something sweet. If I couldn't have drugs or cigarettes candy was the next best thing. Thankfully the commissary supplied candy bars for fifty cents a pop. With all the money I had made from slinging tobacco I would stock up whenever I could. But unfortunately candy never lasted very long. Sometimes I would eat so many Milky Ways I would get sick. My good buddy Susan didn't seem to suffer from the cravings like I did. Maybe it was her athletic background, but she could eat one square of a Hershey's and be satisfied where I would have to eat the whole damn bar.

It was just one more day I had blown through my chocolate when I went to see if Susan had any.

"You got any candy?" I said, standing at the edge of her bunk.

"I already gave you my last piece." A perplexed expression plastered on her face.

"I'm sorry. I'm sorry." I apologized profusely as shame rippled up my spine.

We were only allowed to shop once a week and that meant if I couldn't ration my candy I was out of luck until the following week. And being I could never do anything in moderation, I always ran out.

What I didn't know at the time was sugar has the same effect on the brain as cocaine. It triggers the same reward centers so, it's no wonder I craved it all the time. Candy was escalating my blood sugars and giving me a bit of a high.

In jail, lights would go out at 8:30 right after all the inmates were counted. After that you're not supposed to get up unless you have to go to the bathroom. One night as I laid staring at the bottom bunk, I was gripped by a craving. I imagined the dark brown silky-smooth texture of a square of Hershey's chocolate slowly melting on the tip of my tongue. But memories of candy weren't enough. I wanted the real thing. I knew Smiley was still operating the dorm's black-market store. I dropped down on my hands and knees in my burlap sack shaped nightgown and re-sembling a commando, I crawled across the cold cement floor to the other side of the dorm. Women were glaring at me as I passed but, didn't say anything.

When I got to Smiley, she was reclined in her bunk. She looked down at me and smiled revealing her perfectly white teeth.

"Can I buy some candy?" I whispered.

"How much do you want?" she asked.

"Two Snickers and a Hershey's if ya got it."

Smiley would buy candy all week and wouldn't eat any of it. Instead she'd save it for people like me who had no will power whatsoever. This way she could double her money.

As I laid out my two crumpled dollars on her bunk, she fumbled inside her Ditty bag. When she found it I clutched the candy bars in my hot little hands and shimmied away.

Once back at my bunk I unwrapped the Snickers. When I got a whiff of the sweet smell of chocolate my mouth began to salivate. The first bite was heaven as my teeth sank through the layers of caramel, nuts and milk chocolate. I closed my eyes in an absolute state of glycemic bliss.

I am an addict. I can get hooked on just about anything.

Family Day

After working in the kitchen for months I made a career move to the coveted ceramics department. This was where a dozen hand-picked women would paint statues all day to be sold in the Sheriff's store. At last, I could use all the mad craft skills I had learned while tweaking on meth and paint my way through the rest of my sentence.

One day Officer Lopez, a cool Hispanic cop was escorting six of us to the ceramics department when she came up alongside me and asked, "Don't you have kids Wendy?" "Yeah, I have two boys..." My heart hurt whenever I mentioned them.

"Did you hear about the family day were going to have?"

"What is that?"

"A pilot program with twelve moms who will have contact visits with their kids outside in the courtyard."

Up until then the jail had only allowed mothers to see their kids behind a thick Plexiglas window using tinny phones to talk on. But with the recent research on child-parent separation, psychologists were starting to question the long-term impact on children's developing brains when they saw their moms locked up like that.

A child's sense of safety is already compromised when any parent goes away. I should know, my mother disappeared numerous times until killing herself. This had caused severe anxiety in which I medicated with drugs. Now the medical professionals were finally starting to question the trauma inflicted on children when they were separated from their parents. No shit Sherlock!

I could have told you that. Lopez's keys bounced off her hip as she walked next to me.

"Look, why don't you just fill out the application and see what happens?" Lopez said, using a firm tone.

The nosy inmate in front of me turned her head to see how I was going to respond. I gave her my best 'mind your own business look' causing her to turn away.

"Where do I get the application?"

"I'll drop it off to your dorm myself," Lopez winked.

Later that night I had a disturbing dream:

I am at a park watching my boys play. I am beaming with love as Jerry swings from bar to bar on the jungle gym with Rikki following behind his older brother. When all of the sudden Rikki's fingers start to slip. I try to yell to be careful but I can't get the air into my lungs to form the needed words. I try to run to him but my feet are wedged in the sand like cement. Panic grips me as I watched helplessly and Rikki falls, his arms wind-milling in the air.

At this point I sprang straight up in my bunk sweating and out of breath.

The next day I filled out the application and within a week I was approved for the family day. But now I had another dilemma. How the hell would I get someone to drive Rikki up and wait for him outside while we visited?

When I made my usual Sunday evening collect call, Jennie answered. I spewed out the details of the family day telling her how I had been approved.

"I can't drive all the way up there. I'm getting way too old for that."

"Maybe someone else could bring him up…."

She let out an exasperated exhale and said, "I do think he needs to see his mother. I'll ask Max to bring him."

"Max? You think he will?"

"If I ask him to."

I was convinced Max wouldn't step ten feet near a jail and would make up some excuse why he couldn't do it. But the next Sunday when I called, Jennie said Max had agreed. My jaw came unhinged.

Even though I was still furious with Max, this was the first time in months I actually had something to look forward to. I counted down the days. When the morning finally arrived, Susan used her makeup to help me get presentable. Susan and I were like war buddies who had survived the worst part of our lives together, and as a result had become very close. When she finished all the final touches of lipstick I almost looked like a normal human being again. "You look amazing." Susan stepped back to admire her artistry.

I cringed. "You don't think I need more concealer here?" I touched my blotchy skin.

"Of course not. You look great"

I stared at myself and still didn't see it. I felt so ugly inside.

"What? You don't believe me?"

"Well, sometimes I can't see past my old acne scars."

"I see a gorgeous woman and a mother who gets to see her boy today."

"Thanks Dawg."

As I waited, I had a bad case of butterflies. I kept checking the clock inside the officer station to see what time it was, then would try to sit on the edge of my bunk. I thought Max would flake at the last minute giving me yet another reason to resent him. Then what? I would miss my one and only chance to see one of my boys.

I jumped when my name was called over the PA system. I rushed toward the front of the dorm, nearly slipping on the way. Lopez held the door open for me. "Hey Missy, you better introduce me to your boy." I joined the other mothers in the corridor.

"Are you kidding? This wouldn't have happened if it weren't for you."

Once in the courtyard, it was surreal to see a mini-carnival set up behind the cinderblock and razor-wired walls. It just didn't go with the rest of the scenery. There were booths with smiling trustees who stood by waiting patiently to paint faces or engage kids in game of ring toss. A badminton net had been set up. Jump ropes and rubber balls were scattered across the lawn.

My heart thumped so loudly it echoed in my ears. I shifted back and forth nervously on my feet as I waited in front of the gate. The sun was beating down on my back. A loud hollow sound released the lock and the gate rolled open. There was a stampede of small children escorted by a young pretty blond Sheriff. I was on my tip toes, craning my neck. When I saw Rikki, a lump formed in the back of my throat. He had grown at least an inch since I'd been gone. "Alright ladies, enjoy your visit." Lopez gave us the green light.

I darted over and folded Rikki in my arms. "Hi Mijo" I said, using the Spanish term of endearment. "I'm so happy to see you."

"Hi Mom." He seemed guarded. I planted a big kiss on his flushed, nine-year-old cheek. "I've missed you so, so much."

"I've missed you too Mom." He looked over my shoulder. "So, this is what jail looks like?"

"Well this is actually the nicest part of the jail. It's a bit different on the inside," I pointed to the sinister gray building behind us.

"Is it scary here?" His brown eyes widened with curiosity.

"No, not that bad really…"

"Are there bars and cells everywhere you go?"

"I happen to be in a dorm with a bunch of women. It's kind of like a big slumber party with people you would never actually invite to your house." I smiled.

Rikki giggled. The love in my heart felt like it could spill over. "You want to play some games?" I pointed to the booths.

"Can we just sit down for a while?"

"We can do whatever you like."

The metal chairs were warmed by the afternoon sun and burned the back of my thighs when I sat down. I stared at Rikki. I wanted to take everything in so I could imprint his image and save it for later. He was such a good-looking little guy. His olive skin flawless, long feathery lashes and full puffy lips like his fathers.

"You see your dad much?"

"Not really but he calls me all the time." He gave me a sideways look.

I pressed on. "So, what happened after I went away?"

"At first we got evicted and I stayed in the back of Cat's El Camino with dad until Grandma came and got me."

"You lived in the back of her car?"

I may have been in jail for shooting someone, but it didn't stop me from shamelessly judging Max. What the hell had gotten into him anyway?

Rikki gave me a sideways glance. "I don't want to talk about Dad."

"Okay. I'm sorry. I was just wondering is all."

"When are you getting out Mom?" My insides tightened. It was the same question I'd asked my mother when she was locked up in the State Hospital when I was five. There was a long, tense pause. "Just a few more months is all." I finally said.

His chin fell clear to his chest. "That's so long."

"It will go by fast Rikki... you'll see."

"It's going by really slow..."

I changed the subject. "How do you like living with Grandma?"

"The couch is hard and a clock goes off every hour so it's hard to sleep."

"Geez, I'm sorry Rikki," I draped an arm around his shoulder and pulled him close. "I'm really, really sorry." I hated myself for screwing everything up. I hated that my children had to endure my wreckage.

We silently watched as an enormous inmate the size of a love seat tickled her daughter. The mom's arms were like full legs of lamb that shook like Jell-O as she kneaded her chubby fingers into her little girl's ribs. Another little girl in a pink dress giggled as she ran after a red rubber ball while her mother chased closely behind her. I was surprised to see how happy they all were. Had they all forgotten this was the frigging county jail? Perhaps it's the nature of children to live in the moment, while it's the nature of us adults to live in regret? Only Rikki didn't seem happy and I was to blame for that.

"Where are we going to live when you get out Mom?" Rikki eyes revealed something I'd never seen before. He seemed burdened by life. He wanted reassurance and I couldn't give it to him. I wondered if his innocence was gone forever because of all of my stupidity.

If only I could fast forward into a new life. A life where I had a job with health insurance. Dental insurance. A life where I paid the rent on time and provided for my boys. A life where my car had a full tank of gas. A life where the cupboards were filled with our favorite cereals. A life where the washcloths and towels actually matched. A life full of accomplishments. A life where I kept my word. Couldn't I just bypass all this painful-not-knowing-what-the-fuck-I-was-going-to-do-shit and land somewhere in a future where I didn't loath myself anymore?

I had to be honest with Rikki. No more lying. No more withholding. No more skirting the truth. I would lay it out there. "I don't know where we're going to live Rikki, but I am trying to figure it out."

He looked at me with the saddest brown eyes. "It used to feel like my life was a straight road and now it's all crooked with rocks and stuff in the way," he said softly.

My heart felt crushed. Again. I had made this crocked road. I needed to make it straight. But how? I only had a couple more months before my release date and I desperately needed a place for us to go. Unfortunately, the system didn't provide resources or support for women getting out of jail. There were no drug programs and no counselors at your disposal to assist you with discharge plans. At best we were let out the gate with an insincere 'good luck' from one of the sheriffs. As a result, I was terrified about my release.

Self Esteem

S ybil Brand offered a self-esteem class. While no one would argue that we inmates could use some self-esteem, as far as I knew you couldn't get it in a classroom setting. But I was looking to kill time so I went. As the women entered the school trailer we were greeted by Candy D'Amato, the instructor. In her mid-forties, Candy had jet-black hair and bright blue eyes and was way too friendly for someone as socially awkward as myself. I quickly found a wrap-around desk in the back to get some distance. There were about fifteen other inmates in the class who had come from all over the jail.

"How is everyone doing tonight?" Candy asked.

A few inmates grumbled, while most of us remained silent. I was primed and ready to judge anyone in a position of authority, including a teacher.

"Tonight ladies, I want to talk about passion."

"You mean like getting laid?" said a cat-eyed girl sitting across from me.

Everyone, including Candy laughed. "No, no, no… There's nothing wrong with that, but I'm talking about the things that bring you real joy in your life."

"It's pretty hard to find joy when you're locked up," one inmate declared. No truer words had ever been said.

Candy pressed on. "I understand it would be hard in here but how about another time in your life?"

My thoughts traveled back, flipping through crazy childhood events. I'd admit it wasn't all bad. I used to love summer camp. I loved the time Dad rented a house in Malibu for us. And I especially loved the different animals we had. But most of my memories were overshadowed by my mother's mental illness and measuring Dad's alcohol consumption every night. I thought

Max would be a source of joy for me, but he ended up being another rock in my own crooked path. So, joy? Not so much.

A Hispanic girl interrupted my thoughts. "I used to love to dance," she said.

"So, what did you like about dancing?" Candy asked.

"Ah…maybe because it was the only time I could actually let go?"

"So, you were able to be in the moment?"

"I guess?" The girl shrugged.

"Well I'm sure that was part of it," Candy replied. "As adults, a lot of times we are either worried about the future or regretting something in the past. So maybe when you danced you were able to drop into the present moment."

Candy came around the front of her desk and leaned against it. "Let me tell you how I discovered my passion."

Oh, here we go, I thought, another self-indulgent teacher taking us hostage with stories of privilege. I was regretting coming to class, telling myself that maybe I should have stayed back in the dorm. At least there I might have had a chance to read the current People Magazine that was circulating.

Candy continued to talk. "I remember once as a little girl I was walking with my father, who I adored, and we came across a man who was passed out in the street. I was scared because I thought the man was dead. When I looked up at my father he just looked away. I asked, 'What's wrong with that man Daddy?' and my father said, 'He's a hopeless drunk honey, and he'll never change.'" Candy shook her head, her blue eyes staring off into some distant memory we couldn't see. "Even as a small child, I believed anyone could change if they really wanted to. I decided when I grew up I'd find a way to help the people that my father said would never change. And that one decision has directed my entire life. In fact, that's why I'm standing here today. I believe anyone can change, if they really want to."

I was intrigued not only by Candy's story but by her sincerity as well. I knew this woman was telling us the truth and that she really cared. Candy's vulnerability seemed to trigger the other women to start asking questions. Why did you start teaching in the county jail? What else do you do? We inmates may have been considered outcasts by many, but most of us yearned for deeper meaning in our lives. No one starts out saying, 'When I grow up I'm going to steal, do drugs and go to jail.' Hurt people, hurt other people until they find a way to heal.

When class was over, Candy stood at the door thanking everybody individually for coming. "I really enjoyed the class," I said, barely able to make eye contact.

Candy smiled and said, "I hope you come again."

As a result of attending her classes, I learned that Candy was on the Los Angeles County Commission for Women. And on some nights she would join forces with the Hollywood Police Department trying to convince runaways and prostitutes to go into a local shelter. I also learned from another inmate that Candy belonged to an organization that would sponsor women getting out of jail.

With my release date six weeks away, I still didn't know where I was going when I got out, but asking anyone for help was not in my nature. I thought in order to be strong you had to go it alone. But I had never been so leveled by the circumstances in my life. I was desperate and decided to ask Candy if she knew of anyplace that would take a woman with kids.

I rehearsed what I was going to say over and over again. Ah, "Hi Candy. You probably didn't notice me but I'm the one who sits in the back." The time came and I shifted nervously in my desk all through class. My forehead beaded up with sweat. I was gripped with fear. Could I form the needed words to ask for help or would I go back to the dorm and never utter a word?

When class ended that night, the other inmates filed out of the trailer, while I hovered by Candy's desk. My legs trembled beneath me when Candy looked up.

"Can I help you?" she asked.

"Oh.... um, yes. I, I, was wondering... I heard, well that sometimes you help women getting out?" I stammered.

Candy got up and moved closer, her blue eyes felt like they could see right through me. "Are you in need of help?"

"Well, I, I have a son, two sons actually but my oldest son is in juvie right now and I, and I... have nowhere to go when I get out."

Candy paused. "Where do you live?" she asked.

"My son goes to school in Santa Monica."

Candy nodded. "Tell me something Wendy, do you want to change your life?"

"I do. I really, really do."

"Okay. Let me do a little research and we can talk next week."

"Thank you. Thank you so much." I almost tripped backing out of the classroom so fast.

I was so relieved that there was someone who might actually be able to help me. But no sooner had I hit the bunk then my brain tried to convince me that I had made a huge mistake. What was I thinking anyway? Candy didn't know me from Adam. I'm sure she had enough going on in her own life. No one has time to be burdened with the problems of a stranger. Asking for help was so far out of my realm of my personal experience and I started feeling like I had made a fool of myself.

Several days passed with me in a perpetual state of anxiety. I kept it well hidden because that's what I had been doing all my life. The clock ticked away, my release date was getting closer when I was told to report to the attorney's room.

When I arrived, I handed the trustee my hall pass. After reading it the trustee said, "Someone is waiting for you in there," she pointed to the adjacent room. I turned and opened the door. Candy was sitting at one of the small tables leafing through papers.

My heart thumped as I walked over and lowered myself in the seat across from her. "I got some good news, Wendy." Candy smiled.

"Really?"

"I talked to some ladies who I'm involved with and they want to help you."

My hand shot up to my mouth. "You're kidding me."

Candy shook her head smiling. "No. It's absolutely true."

"Oh my God. I can't believe it. I, I, I've been so stressed out."

"Well you don't have to stress anymore." Candy patted me gently on my hand. "But first I have to find someplace that will take you and your son."

"Do you think you'll be able to find somewhere?"

"There is a place called Clare Foundation that has women and children's apartments. I'm going to reach out to them to see if they have any beds."

I bit on my lower lip. My eyes teared up. "Thank you so much for helping me."

In jail I had been feeling more like a mannequin than someone of flesh and bone. Gripped with stress on a daily basis, my jaw was tight. But with Candy's news, I was filled with new hope and it seemed that all of my muscles instantly relaxed.

Roll It Up

W ith my release date closing in, I could barely sleep. I kept future tripping. The time seemed to crawl. Day 15. I was filled with self-doubt. Day 10. I couldn't sleep. How would I ever be able to stay sober out there? Day 5. My stomach was tied up in knots and I could barely eat.

When the actual morning arrived, I was pacing back and forth looking at the clock. I was terrified. What was I going to do? How would I support myself? My thoughts slammed into each other like bugs in a jar.

I flinched when, "Adamson, roll it UP!" blasted over the PA system. I immediately sprang into action, peeling off the sheets from my thin mattress while Susan stood silently at the foot of my bunk. I hated saying goodbye to people and had been dreading it for days.

"It's not going to be the same in here without you," Susan said, lowering her head.

"I wish I could take you with me, girl." I stuffed the sheets into the pillow case and looked at her. "We'll just have to hang when you get out of this hell hole."

We both knew the chances of us ever seeing each other were slim. She was from Orange County and I was from LA and there might as well been an entire ocean between us even if it was only sixty miles away.

"Maybe we should go into business selling tobacco or something?" Susan said.

"I don't think we'd be happy unless we were breaking some sort of law."

Susan laughed with eyes that glistened with tears.

I moved forward to hug her, breaking the 'no physical contact' rule. I could feel her shoulders tremble. It made me uncomfortable. "I have to go." I stepped back. "I'll write to you."

"Please…" she said.

I took a deep breath and walked away before I lost my shit. Taking my bedding to the front of the dorm, I told the officer I was ready to go. One last time I turned around and waved. That was the last time I ever saw Susan.

Exhaling, I walked at a fast clip to admissions and reported to the on-duty officer who checked my wristband to make sure I was not some imposter trying to escape. She gave me my street clothes, I signed a series of papers and before I knew it I was in the outside lobby slipping loose coins into the cigarette machine.

When I stepped outside it was like emerging from a movie theater. I had to adjust to a different reality. I blinked back the brightness of the sun. The sky was a robin egg blue with soft white clouds drifting by. I lit up a cigarette and blew a defiant puff of smoke towards Sybil Brand. *You won't be seeing this girl ever again assholes!* But by the third drag I was dizzy and snuffed the cigarette out beneath my tennis shoe.

I waited by the curb when a fire-engine red Mustang with sleek black racing strips pulled up. The tinted passenger window went down and Candy leaned over, "Hey Wendy, hop on in."

"Oh, hi Candy. I didn't realize that was you." The smell of leather and expensive perfume permeated the air as I crawled in. "Some fancy car you got here."

Candy laughed. "It was a birthday present to myself."

I held my property envelope on my lap, wondering what it would be like to give yourself a present like that.

"Let's get out of here." Candy stepped on the gas and we peeled away.

The car had so much horsepower under the hood it was unsettling. I found my hand reaching for the dashboard every few seconds as if I was bracing for a crash. Once on the freeway, I watched the moving landscapes, each building, each landmark, putting more distance between me and jail. Between me and that other life.

An hour later we pulled up in front of Jennie's little yellow house with its tall black iron gates that wrapped around the entire perimeter. If there had been razor wire I might have felt right at home.

Candy looked at me with the kindest eyes "How you feeling about this?"

"Nervous..."

"We won't stay very long."

As absurd as it may sound now, the plan had always been for me to pick up Rikki the day I got out. Maybe Jennie didn't want any more time to go by that might give me the opportunity to get in more trouble or maybe she wanted her life back, in either case I never questioned it because I missed my boys so much. We got out and Candy followed me up the path and as I rang the doorbell I let out a long sigh. A moment later Rikki answered, in high-top sneakers, a t-shirt, and basketball shorts. I folded his lanky body into my arms, "Hi Rikki I'm so happy to see you."

"Hi Mom." I must have been holding too tight because he squirmed away.

"This is Candy, the woman I told you about," I gestured with my hand.

"Nice to meet you, young man," Candy said. Rikki's small hand disappeared in hers.

"Hello." He acted shy and turned back to me. "Grandma's waiting inside."

We stepped into the living room and everything was the same. The smell of years of homemade tortillas and crushed chilies were baked into the walls. There was the same brown and black plaid couch with its matching chair. White crocheted doilies Jennie had made when her fingers were nimble covered most of the furniture. A television sat in the corner with a VHS player with stacks of old movies alongside it. Glass cabinets with shelves of ceramic angels, owl figurines, birds, roosters and elephants were everywhere you looked. Jennie was in her late seventies and had spent a great deal of her life collecting things. She found some secret satisfaction from arranging, re-arranging and dusting each of her little statuettes. That's where we were different. To me her collections represented more housework, something I despised. Jennie could spend an entire day joyfully organizing it all.

"Hello Wendy," Jennie gave me a quick hug.

"Hi Jennie."

Her long salt and pepper hair framed her weather-beaten face. She was wearing an ankle-length floral dress that she probably made herself. I was afraid that she was mad at me. And who could blame her if she was. I had been a terrible daughter-in-law who over-relied on her to take care of my kids. After all the introductions were said and done everyone sat down and engaged in superficial talk until Jennie asked, "What's the plan?"

Candy answered her. "The organization I work with is going to help Wendy get on her feet. So, tonight Rikki and Wendy can stay in a motel, but tomorrow I've set up an interview with a women and children's center nearby to see if she can get an apartment there."

Jennie had a hint of a smile. "That sounds very promising."

"I really think Wendy wants to change."

"I hope she does. At least for the sake of her children," Jennie said.

I momentarily disappeared like I did when my dad talked about me with the nuns, the cops or whoever I was in trouble with at the time.

I flinched when the phone rang. Jennie pushed herself up to go answer it. She kept her back toward us and spoke in soft tones. I was a bit surprised when Jennie turned to me and said "Max wants to talk to you," extending the receiver in her hand.

My jaw must have hit the floor. "He wants to talk to me?"

I got up and took the phone from Jennie and held it to my ear.

"Hello?"

"Hey Wendy, how's it going?" Max said.

"Well it's going, I guess." Everyone was watching me.

"Yeah my mom told me you were picking Rikki up today so I thought I'd give you a call."

"For what?"

"Well, I, I, just wanted to say that um, um, I don't want any trouble…."

"What do you mean by trouble?" My stomach clenched in a knot.

"Cat and I are just trying to move on and…"

I don't remember what else he said but I got a sense he was still using drugs, or clearly he might have been more concerned about where his ex-wife and son were going to live. He was only worried about me coming after the two of them. The sting of his words morphed into rage, but as everyone in that room watched me, I hardened my insides and didn't let on to the crushing pain that rippled through my entire body.

"Don't worry Max. I've moved on with my life too, you know." My knuckles gripped the phone so hard it's a wonder I didn't crush the receiver with my hand.

"Oh. Great… I just wanted to make sure we had an understanding is all." I could have sworn I heard the hint of disappointment in his voice that I had moved on.

After saying goodbye, I tucked my feelings away and joined the others. There was a tension hanging in the air or maybe the tension was coming from deep inside me? All I knew was I wanted to get the hell out of there.

"Does Rikki have some clothes to take with him?" I asked.

Jennie handed me a brown shopping bag she had prepared. "When you're settled into your new place you can come get the rest of his things." Turning to Rikki, she said, "I made you some burritos in case you get hungry later." She handed Rikki a brown lunch bag.

"Thanks Grandma," he said as she kissed him on the cheek.

"I can't tell you how grateful I am for taking care of him all this time."

"Look Wendy, all I want is for you to be happy and for you to be a mother to your children now."

I wanted to take on my responsibilities, so I nodded and smiled. We hugged and said good bye and I told her I would be back soon.

A few minutes later we were checking into a small room at the Palm Motel. Candy told us she'd be back in the morning to pick us up.

Our room had two double beds with thick maroon curtains that blocked out any light. But what I remember most was the realization that I could walk down to the corner liquor store and get a bottle of wine and no one could stop me. Why didn't I? Because Rikki was depending on me, so instead I chained smoked while he watched sitcoms from the other bed. Little did he know his mother was fighting the urge to run away. After all, I was an expert at wearing masks.

The Interview

The next morning Candy came and took us to the Clare Foundation in her red Mustang. My heart raced as we walked into the dilapidated storefront building. I almost wanted to throw up. What if I didn't pass this interview? What if I said the wrong thing? What if we ended up living on the streets? Then what?

Slogans like *One Day at a Time* and *Easy Does It* hung on all the walls. I knew this was where they held those dreaded twelve-step meetings I despised. I had been to some of them in prison, jail and hospitals but I only went for the cookies and donuts, not because I thought it could actually work for me. If I had to go to meetings to have a place to live I would, but I had no plans on joining a cult.

We walked down the hallway until we came to a small office where a middle-aged woman with dark hair shuffled through paperwork on her desk.

Candy tapped on the door. "Do you know where we could find Ruth?"

"You just found her." The woman stood up and extended her hand.

After introductions Ruth invited us to have a seat. A puff of dust escaped from the second-hand couch as we plopped down and Ruth sat across from us in a swivel chair. Against one wall were rows of self-help books such as, *"The Road Less Traveled"* and, *"Women Who Love Too Much."* Many of them I had read, but never found any of them to actually help. In all fairness, that could have been because I was getting high all the time.

Ruth said to Candy, "How wonderful that your organization helps women getting out of jail."

Candy nodded. "I only wish we could help more."

"How do you decide which ones?"

"Well, I try to gauge sincerity but there are no guarantees." Candy looked over at me. "But I believe Wendy here is really wanting to turn her life around."

My gaze was cast down, locked onto a dust ball under the desk.

"Could I talk to Wendy alone for a few minutes?" Ruth asked. Right about then I wanted to sink deeper into the sofa and disappear. I was afraid Ruth would ask questions that would instantly disqualify me. It was my core belief that the odds in my life had always been stacked against me. Always had been and always would be.

Candy stood up. "Rikki why don't we go outside and play?"

"Can we sit in your car?"

"I'll tell you what young man, I'll even let you sit behind the wheel."

Excited, Rikki jumped up and down. When the door closed behind them there was a moment of awkward silence. I stuffed my hands under my thighs to stop them from shaking.

"You know I've been sober fifteen years now, Wendy?"

"Oh... I didn't know that."

I couldn't understand how anyone could stay sober unless they were locked up. At some point, Ruth reached over and picked up a picture frame of a teenage boy, "This was my son. He died from an overdose when I was just five years sober."

"Oh geez, I'm so sorry...."

"I was an alcoholic while he was growing up and felt guilty for not being there for him. After he died I was so depressed, all I could do was sleep."

I thought losing a child was the worst possible thing that could happen to someone. I didn't know the words to make Ruth feel better about her loss.

Ruth continued, "I decided that since I wasn't there for Frank, I would make amends by opening up the women and children center so I could help as many other kids as possible.

I figure if you can help one mother get sober it helps the entire family." She paused and let out a long sigh. "So Wendy, can you tell me why you want to be sober?"

Here it is, I thought. The trick question that could get me voted off the island. My breath caught in my chest.

"Well, I just, well, I, I don't know, I just, ummm, I'm tired… and I want, I want a better life." I couldn't even finish a complete sentence. I felt pathetic.

Ruth leaned forward and patted me gently on my knee, "Wendy, the place is all yours," she said.

"Really? We can move it?"

"Yes, we just need to have you sign some forms and go over a few rules."

My shoulders dropped from around my ears. "Oh my God. Thank you. Thank you so much."

Ruth explained how rent would be four-hundred dollars and that Candy's organization had agreed to pay for the first two months. After that I could either find a job or get on welfare. Since I had a rap sheet and no marketable skills to speak of, I would end up getting on welfare. Ruth went on to tell me about the 10 p.m. curfew and how I had to attend three manda-tory 12-step meetings a week as well as a house meeting every Saturday morning. She also explained that I'd have a housemate whose name was Lara. She had a five-year-old son with Down Syndrome. As she listed the rules and regulations my head went up and down like a bobble doll. I would have agreed to anything just to keep Rikki and I off the streets.

Afterward Candy bought us enough groceries for a week and drove us to the center, which was a tan six-unit apartment building on a busy boulevard in Culver City. Holding the bags of groceries, we walked up the stairs in the back. Since no one answered the door when I knocked, I used the key Ruth gave me. I think it's safe to say we were all shocked at the state of the living room. There were toys scattered on the floor and ashtrays overflowing with cigarette butts on the coffee table.

"Geez Mom this place is a mess," Rikki said, stating the obvious.

Candy and I looked at each other before making our way to the kitchen that had dirty dishes piled in the sink and a crusty pan of old macaroni and cheese sitting on top of the stove.

We set down the groceries and Candy said, "Let's go see your room."

The bedroom was bare bones with white walls, twin beds and two unmatched dressers. Candy, the optimist said, "Once you fix it up it'll feel more like home."

"Some pictures on the wall will totally perk things up," I said, trying to follow her lead.

"I better be hitting the road," Candy said. "It's getting late."

Once we said our goodbyes at the door, I asked, "How can I pay you back for all you've done?"

"Just stay sober and that will be payment enough."

"I will," I said, not sure that I could keep that promise.

When Rikki and I were alone I felt completely out of place. This wasn't my home. The evidence was all around me in the toys, magazines and even the macaroni on the stove. It all belonged to someone else. What was I doing there anyway? Why did I keep ending up living in places I didn't belong? And the fact that I was dragging my son along for my "joyride" of a life, only made it so much worse.

Later, Rikki and I were eating turkey sandwiches at the kitchen table when the back door flew open. It was my new roommate, Lara, who had a square jaw and short blond hair with two-inches of black roots. She was wearing shorts and sandals and her son, Jake, had slanted eyes and a large forehead. His mouth fell wide open. He squirmed out of his mother's grip and ran to Rikki wrapping his little arms around his legs. Not knowing what to do, I just sat there, until Lara bent over and unlocked his fingers. "Oh, honey, I'm so sorry but whenever Jake sees another kid he wants to play."

Desperately wanting to make a good first impression, I said, "He doesn't mind. Do you Rikki?"

Rikki didn't say anything but his burrowing, brown eyes said; 'Yes, Mom, I do mind. In fact, I mind very much. I mind that you've been gone for a year. I mind that Dad and my brother aren't with us anymore. And I really, really mind that I have to live with these strangers in a filthy house.'

Probation

I dropped Rikki off at school and headed over to the probation department, which was several blocks away. The judge had given me three years of supervised probation and I was now several weeks in. That meant I had to report every month, give random urine samples and have one-on-one visits with my probation officer.

As I pushed the double doors open with my shoulder, I entered a huge waiting area with rows of fluorescent lights that buzzed overhead. A Hispanic gang-banger wearing waist-high khakis and a white t-shirt stood against the far wall. A girl with curly hair glared at me as I made my way to the reception desk where a large woman sat with shoulders hunched up to her ears.

I handed her my paperwork and said, "I have an appointment with Mrs. Jones."

Barely looking up she shoved a form across the desk. "Fill this out and I'll let her know you're here."

I sat down at one of the long tables and answered the questions with a three-inch, miniature golf pencil. The questions asked, Had I been working? Had I looked for work? Had I been arrested? All things a probation officer would need to know to track your progress or lack there in. I was so nervous my stomach was doing somersaults. Ten minutes later a large doughy woman with a mess of gray hair called my name. I walked towards her, determined to make a good first impression, but all she said was, "Come with me," curling a finger before she turned around.

Mrs. Jones' large frame lumbered down the narrow hall. I had to walk slow, so I wouldn't be swallowed up by her massive girth. Toward the end of the corridor I followed her into a partitioned cubby hole of an office. "Have a seat." She turned sideways to get in behind her desk.

Mrs. Jones reviewed my two-inch thick file. On the wall behind her was a picture of a sunny-side egg frying in a Teflon pan which said, *This Is Your Brain on Drugs.* It seemed such a lame old fashioned way to talk to drug addicts. On top of her desk was a circular Rolodex with a phone that had red flashing lights lit like a Christmas tree. I crossed my arms in front of my chest waiting for her to address me.

"You have quite the record here, Wendy." Mrs. Jones peered over her rectangle glasses with her forehead scrunched up.

Not knowing how to respond I just shrugged.

"So, what's going to be different this time?"

If I were to tell her what I really thought I would have said, 'nothing is going to be different.' I would have told her I was terrified of doing my life without drugs. That chaos was my comfort zone so why not just blow everything up? I would have explained that I felt like a damaged human being who needed intensive therapy. But since I couldn't afford it, and the system didn't offer it, I'd probably end up getting high. But I didn't say any of those things and instead pulled out a personality from my trusted Rolodex to suit the situation.

"I'll stay at Clare women and children center until I can get my own place."

"How about a job?"

"I'm filing for welfare until I figure out what I can do for work."

She eyed me suspiciously, and said, "You can go to the unemployment office and check their listings."

"Okay, sure. I can do that…" I said, pretending again.

"Have you talked to your ex-husband?"

I didn't tell Mrs. Jones that Max had called a couple times promising to come visit Rikki. I didn't mention how Rikki had waited by the window for hours and his Dad never showed. I didn't go into how Rikki was so mad that he kicked the football clear across the living room before storming off to our room. I didn't say how angry I was because Max was still affecting my life even though he wasn't in it anymore. It was none of her business, so I lied. "No. I haven't talked to him at all."

"I think it's best if you don't," Mrs. Jones said with a stern tone. "Judging from your file, you two seem to get into a lot of trouble together."

"Yes ma'am."

Sliding a paper slip across her desk, she said, "I want you to call this number every night after 7:00 o'clock. If you hear 'yellow' on the outgoing message that means you need to come in the next day for a urinalysis."

"Yes ma'am."

"And by the way, if you give a dirty test you'll go straight back to jail."

I took the paper and smiled while sending Mrs. Jones a thousand fuck you's inside my head.

Sober Living

I found life excruciating. I had been out for nearly two months and without some sort of drug pulsing through my system. Before I had beaten back the terror and fear through self-medicating. Sober, I felt like one raw nerve. Everything was hard for me to do. I only went to the welfare department because I needed a check and food stamps. Taking the bus, going to the market and just carrying on a normal conversation with someone felt like a foreign country to me.

And while one would think with all the jails, detoxes and mental institutions I had been in that I'd be able to endure any personality, that was not the case with my roommate, Lara. I couldn't stand her. She was messy and had her stuff spread out all over the place. She'd also get on the phone every night, her voice shrill, while Rikki and I tried to watch television. Did I say anything to her? No. I told myself she was there first and I was the one infringing on her territory, but inside I was seething with resentment and contempt. Not just for her, but at my inability to function in the world.

The twelve-step meetings I was required to attend were difficult to navigate as well. But at least they offered childcare run by a Latina woman, Gloria, who had straight black hair, hazel eyes and a warm laugh. She loved the kids and would stand outside the family center greeting each of them with a smile and a hug.

"Well hello their young man," Gloria said, bending down on one knee. "Good to see you again Rikki."

Clearly as shy as his mother, he smiled and looked away. When I leaned over to kiss Rikki on the cheek he batted his hand in the air reminding me not to embarrass him in front of all the other kids.

"I'll see you in an hour then," I said, and went to the parking lot to smoke a cigarette. With extreme social phobia, I tried avoiding interactions with anyone. When I was done I crushed the cigarette under foot and went inside.

The meeting room had rows of metal chairs, a table with literature and stupid, black framed slogans that hung on smoke-stained-walls. As everyone settled in, I grabbed a handful of cookies and found a chair with my back against the wall. I always felt a little safer if I could keep an eye on everyone.

I was learning that many of the members in these meetings had shared some of the same humiliations and heartbreak that I had experienced. They claimed to have tried every known method to stop using drugs or drinking themselves to death. But prayer, therapy, cleanses, rehabs and their own sorry willpower hadn't worked. Some of them even tried killing themselves but obviously had failed at that too. Even though there were similarities, I still thought none of them had suffered as much as me. And surely if they ever heard my story they'd get a glimpse at what a real bottom looks like. But until I found the nerve to open my mouth, I'd just have to sit through an hour of bone-crushing boredom eating my Chips Ahoy.

Crumbs fell onto my lap as I scanned the room for any cute guys. There was a tattooed biker dude that sat on the other side of the room every week. He wasn't exactly handsome but he wasn't ugly either. He had deep creases in his brow that made him seem in a perpetual state of anger. His outsides seemed to match my insides. But could I actually date a guy with a ponytail and a swastika tattooed on his arm? When he caught me staring I half-smiled from across the room. He just looked away. Talk about demoralizing, I couldn't even get a smile from the angry biker in a room full of losers. I sank a little lower in my seat and shoved the rest of the cookie into my mouth.

The speaker was a girl in her mid-thirties with spikey hair, black nail polish and a silver studded choker. She wore her defiance on her skin in an intricate web work of tattoos up and down her arms. I related when she said, "My parents were never there and I pretty much raised myself."

My hearing lasered in as she went on, "Later I looked for guys who would make me feel safe in what I thought to be a scary world."

In spite of myself I identified with this rocker chick. I had always looked to Max to make me feel safe. That's what attracted me to him in the first place. As I listened to her share it was like she was holding up a mirror for me. Through identification I was learning things about myself that I couldn't otherwise see. But as soon as my new ally mentioned the word 'God,' a steel door slammed shut inside my brain. Whenever anyone spoke of a higher power, I assumed they were talking about the bearded man in the sky. The same omnipotent man the nuns said loved me unconditionally, unless I broke one of the commandments and then He would cast me to hell. I thought it was all major-league-bullshit when I was a kid and I certainly wasn't going to buy it now.

After the meeting was over everyone held hands in a circle to say the Serenity Prayer and afterward they chanted, "it works if you work it." I found this all very cultish and as soon as my hands were free I rushed to the parking lot to smoke another cigarette. I was terrified of people. I was terrified of everything and had no frigging clue why. This was not a life I was used to. Being sober was an unnatural act for me and it made me want to tear the skin right off the bone.

Panic Attack

I thought about getting high constantly. Just because I'd stopped doing drugs, didn't mean I'd stopped thinking about them. Cravings surrounded me like my own personal weather system hovering above my tortured head. There was no mistaking that drugs had gotten me into a lot of trouble, but I was trying to convince myself that booze had never been a problem for me. The temptation was everywhere. It felt like the whole city was an alcohol advertisement, whether it was commercials with lovers sipping Chardonnay, or billboards of gorgeous young people at a keg party on the beach. I felt deprived and thought everyone was having a good time except me.

To combat my urges, I tried to stay on a routine. Every morning I took Rikki on two buses to a school in Santa Monica and took two buses to get back. Once in the apartment, I'd watch reruns of sitcoms and chain smoke until just before Rikki was getting out of school, and then I'd take two buses again to pick him up. I thought this was my penance for screwing up everyone's lives.

I remember one particular morning while Rikki was at school, I had to mentally armor-up just to get myself to the market to buy some much-needed food. Sometimes just being in the pedestrian world without a buffer could cause me severe anxiety. I told myself, *'you can do this, girl. Just get in and get out. Don't diddle daddle anywhere near the liquor aisle.'*

I managed to walk the two blocks to the grocery store, grabbed a cart and entered the automatic doors, making sure I didn't make eye contact with anyone. I headed straight for the cheapest processed food to give me the most bang for my food stamp buck. Frozen waffles, hot pockets and of course, TV dinners like I had in my formative years.

I was sailing through my shopping list when I happened upon a display of Budweiser six packs stacked in a pyramid pointing towards heaven itself. I slowed down. My eyes lingered on the glossy picture of a tantalizing, glass of golden liquid with beads of sweat on its side. *Boy that sure looks good,* I thought. *It's so hot outside today and a beer would certainly hit the spot. I mean, it's not like its hard liquor and besides, no one would have to know.* Fortunately, I recognized what was happening and shook my head in an attempt to free myself from the trance of effective advertising.

As I headed down the cereal aisle, my hands gripped the cart tight. So many colorful boxes to choose from. I felt overwhelmed. My eyes darted back and forth down the long aisle trying to decide which one I should buy. What cereal did the other moms at Rikki's school get for their kids? Are Corn Flakes more nutritious than Frosted Flakes or should I be making Rikki oatmeal and fruit in the mornings? But Rikki told me he wanted Cocoa Pebbles, which was pure sugar disguised as food.

My fingers started to tingle. My heart thumped inside my chest. Blood raced through my veins. *How pathetic,* I thought. I was a grown woman who couldn't decide what cereal to buy her son. I looked back and forth to make sure no one was watching me because I was starting to freak out. It felt like the aisles were closing in on me and I was going to get crushed in a tsunami of cardboard boxes and genetically modified food. The fluorescent lights burned my skin. I had to get the fuck out of there and I had to get out immediately.

I turned, leaving my cart behind and rushed toward freedom. I almost crashed into the automatic doors because they couldn't spit me out fast enough. Once in the parking lot I went around the corner of the building to hide. I leaned over and placed my hands on my knees. I was hyperventilating but it felt more like a heart attack. The whiteness of the sun blinded me. Oh my God. Oh my God. Oh my God. I'm going to die. An elderly woman suspiciously gazed at me as she walked by with her cart. Then somehow in the recesses of my mind, I remembered what I'd heard in a meeting once. When you're feeling anxious, remember to breathe. I took a deep, slow inhale and held it in. I did it again. And again. And again. Until finally my heart started to slow down. My vision became normal again. I leaned against the cement wall and looked around.

It was a full-blown panic attack. Going to the market sober was much harder than I ever imagined it would be. Man, I could really use that beer.

Slippery Slope

Ihad already been out several months when Max finally came to see Rikki. He had promised to visit on the phone but flaked so many times I was surprised when I saw him walking up the path. He had the same boyish bounce in his step that he had when we were sixteen. It took me back to a time when our love was new and I believed we'd be together for the rest of our lives. But I was much smarter now.

He wore dark shades, a baseball cap and looked ghostly thin. I was shocked when I was hit with an avalanche of emotions. Anger. Love. Hate. Desire. Resentment. All swirling around inside me at once.

"Dad, Dad you came!" Rikki ran up and threw his arms around him.

"Of course, I did. I needed to see my little man."

I swallowed the stone stuck in the back of my throat.

Max stood up. "You're looking mighty fine there, girl." He eyed me up and down.

"I gained a lot of weight in jail." My face was hot.

"A little butter never hurt anyone and besides, you were way too skinny before."

Max was a flirt and that hadn't changed one bit.

"So how do you like living here?" he asked.

"Oh, you know. It's okay but I have to go to twelve-step meetings a lot."

"Not so bad for getting your own place to live."

"Where are you living these days?"

"Cat and I are staying with some friends."

I took a deep breath and exhaled slowly. Just hearing Cat's name felt like an icepick going straight through me. It brought back the intense feelings of betrayal I felt when I realized

Cat had slithered in and stole the man from right under my nose. I hated her for that. And besides, I was still holding on to a thread of hope that Max and I could get back together one day. Hearing her name burst that bubble completely. Rikki looked up and said, "Dad will you play catch with me?"

"Sure Mijo, where's your ball?"

"I'll go get it upstairs," Rikki turned and ran up the steps while Max moved a little closer.

"I brought you a surprise," he whispered, pressing a small folded triangle paper into my hand. "Something to celebrate getting out of jail." He winked.

My heart pounded against my ribs. My mouth salivated. I knew instantly what it was and every cell in my body was screaming with excitement. Just having that shit in my hand caused my stomach to churn with heated anticipation. My throat constricted. My forehead beaded up with sweat. Drugs were kryptonite and it felt like I didn't have a choice. I wanted it, needed it and would have walked across hot coals just to get high.

"Thank you so much." I tucked it into my bra close to my heart just as I heard Rikki's footsteps coming down the stairs. I turned and smiled. I was a master at wearing masks. A master of deception… even with my kids.

"You ready to play Dad?"

"You bet I am."

"I have to go to the bathroom," I said, taking the stairs two at a time.

Lara wasn't home that day when I laid out a dollar bill, a business card and mirror on the back of the tank like party favors. No one saw me as I straddled the toilet backwards and tapped the white crystal powder onto the mirror. I used a business card given to me by some stranger in a twelve-step meeting to carve out a thin white line. I rolled a dollar bill into a tight cylinder and just like a human vacuum cleaner, in one sweep, snorted the chemicals up my nose. It burned my sinuses. It burned my brain. The blood rushed through my veins. My lungs were on fire as a surge of dopamine turned me inside out. The chemical embrace gave me a reprieve from the onslaught of responsibilities I felt burdened with. I wiped the mirror clean with the back of my sleeve. Now, I was ready to take on the world.

As I came down the steps, Rikki was busy playing ball with his father. He was unaware of the fact that my heart was pounding inside my chest like a drum. He was unaware that I was trying to act normal. Instead, we all pretended like things were good again that day. We didn't talk about Cat or jail or how we had blown up our lives. I made turkey sandwiches just the way Max used to like them with plenty of mayonnaise. I filled up Tupperware glasses with strawberry Kool Aid but didn't eat anything myself. Eventually Max said it was time to go, so we all said goodbye and gave hugs and Max promised to be back the following week.

It wasn't until much later when Rikki was sleeping that I was flooded with a tsunami of regrets. As I lay there staring at the cottage cheese ceiling, the drugs began to dissipate and a wave of despair washed-up inside my brain. How had I so easily succumbed to snorting that shit without giving it a second thought? How come I didn't stop to consider the risks I was taking or the consequence? I didn't think about getting kicked out or being called in for a urinalysis by my probation officer. I didn't think about hurting my kids if I ended up going back to jail. I felt like a loser. A dirty, filthy drug addict loser. Nothing had changed and nothing ever would. Fuck. I hated myself for that. Rikki sighed from across the room. He looked innocent sleeping with his mouth slightly parted as he breathed in and out.

Why couldn't I be strong for him?

Why couldn't I "just say no?"

Why did I always end up hurting the people I claimed to love? Shouldn't my love for them be enough to make me stop?

The rest of the night ticked slowly by while remorse flooded in. And lucky me, I was awake to experience it all. I was awake for the sweats, the chills, and I was awake for the fallout of a thousand voices of self-hatred berating me inside my brain.

After hours of lying there my thoughts circled back to where they always did when I encountered a dark place. Wouldn't it be better if I just ended it all like my mother did? Wouldn't everyone be better off if I were dead?

The Room Mate

Luckily, I didn't get called in by my probation officer for a urinalysis but there were other problems brewing on the old Soberosa. It all came to a nasty head one evening when Rikki and I were watching Fresh Prince of Bel Air. Jake was playing with his toys and Lara was on the phone working herself up into a frenzy like she did every night.

Rikki was lying on the floor in his pajamas and I sat behind him on the couch. Lara's voice could get so shrill it was like a nail being dragging across a chalkboard.

Rikki turned, and said, "Mom I can't hear the television."

"Turn it up, then." I shrugged.

When he did, it helped drown out the sound of her voice but within seconds Lara countered with, "Can you *please* turn the television down?"

"We can't hear the television out here, Lara."

"Alright, I'll keep it down."

I gave Rikki a nod and he lowered it. A few minutes passed and Rikki asked, "Where did Jake go?"

Jake was a regular Houdini and whenever his mom was on the phone he would silently slip out the front door and head to the corner liquor store where he'd grab a fistful of candy off the shelf. It happened all the time and while I had joined in the frantic searches before, I was growing tired of it.

"Lara! Jake is gone again!"

Stopping mid-sentence, Lara hung up the phone. "Where did he go?"

"I don't know. He was playing here just a minute ago."

Lara screamed as she ran out the door, "Jake! Jake! Jake!"

I lit another cigarette and took a deep inhale.

"Why doesn't she watch him?" Rikki asked.

I shrugged. "She's busy, I guess."

A few minutes later Lara came back in the door, dragging Jake's hand with her lips pulled tight.

"You could have stopped him!" Lara said, out of breath.

"We didn't see him leave," I snapped.

"How could you not see him? You were right here."

My eyes narrowed as we stared each other down in some Mexican stand-off of wills. My experience in jail told me not to back down so, I held my ground. "If you weren't so busy talking on the phone every night you might be able to watch your own son."

Her hand shot straight up to her mouth. "Oh my God!"

Jake was still smiling as his eyes darted back and forth watching us.

"Every night you are on that damn phone."

Her voice jumped on octave. "You have no idea what it's like to have a son with a handicap."

"I would think that would be even more reason to pay attention to him."

I stood up and motioned to Rikki. "Let's go."

Once inside our room I slammed the door. Rikki and I sat across from each other on our twin beds. "When are we going to get out of here, Mom?" he asked.

"I don't have the money or we would have been gone." It was three months and I barely had anything left after I paid the four hundred dollars rent from my welfare check. It felt like I'd never get out of there.

"I hate it here." Rikki crawled under the covers, his head hitting the pillow hard.

I could barely swallow over the lump in my throat. Jake, as clever as he was, may have been able to slip out the front door but, I was feeling more and more trapped every day.

Holey Shoes

One morning, we were running late and Rikki was still busy getting ready when he said, "Mom, both my shoes have holes in them." He flipped over his high-tops to show me the bottom of the soles that were worn clear through.

"I'm sorry but you'll have to wait."

"But the kids will make fun of me at school."

"I don't have the money right now Rikki..."

He interrupted me. "Can you ask Grandma?"

"She already loaned me money for food so, no."

"But the kids are so mean..."

The pressure of keeping up with the privileged kids that attended Santa Monica School District was already high, but to add to that was the brand-driven shoes that were loaded with hidden meanings for kids. Fame-based marketing used athletes to maximize their sales and if you didn't have on your favorite basketball player's sneakers or if you weren't making an anti-fashion statement with a pair of Converse, you could be labeled an irredeemable loser. While I didn't know any of this at the time, Rikki was well aware of it all.

"What if I line the inside of your shoes with cardboard?" I went totally old school on him.

"That's a really stupid idea Mom."

I let out a long sigh. It was a stupid idea and I had plenty more where that came from. "Let's get going or we'll miss the bus."

Rikki swung his stuffed, backpack over his shoulder and we silently made our way to the corner. I flinched when the Big Blue Bus rolled up, making a loud hissing sound as it released its air brakes. We climbed up the steps and I dropped coins in the slot for the both of us. Rikki and I found a seat half way down the aisle.

On the ride over I noticed a polished dark-haired woman in a power suit marking papers with a pen. With her black pumps and leather briefcase she was the embodiment of success. I was constantly comparing everyone's outsides to my insides, and as a result, I was always coming up short. That's just how my mind worked back then.

She must have felt me watching because she looked up with dazzling hazel eyes and smiled. Embarrassed, I turned and gazed out the window. For the first time I noticed there were dark clouds rolling across the sky. Was it supposed to rain today, I wondered? I had dressed Rikki in a hoodie and basketball shorts but it was way too late to go back and have him put on something else. Instead, I convinced myself he would be fine. After all, it never rains in sunny Southern California.

Once at the playground I watched as Rikki joined the other kids. And indeed, a lot of them were wearing Air Jordans, Vans and Nikes. I was pretty damn sure none of these kids slept in the same room with their jailhouse mothers. *Rich little fuckers*, I thought before I walked away.

Two more buses and I was back to the Soberosa, chain-smoking and watching reruns of I Love Lucy. As I sat there contemplating the pathetic nature of my life, I started feeling depressed. Again. It seemed when I had any down time, the sadness in my belly would rise up to remind me, 'Hey you, I'm still there. You're not getting off that easy.'

I was sinking into despair when I heard the first roll of thunder. It shook the entire building. I looked out the window and it was dark. Regret took hold of me. I knew I should have dressed Rikki in warmer clothes. A few minutes later, sheets of rain were pounding on the roof. I lit another cigarette to try to calm myself.

Later that afternoon as I stood under the awning at Rikki's school, I secretly checked out all the other moms that were waiting for their kids. There was a young blond with a Gucci bag hanging from her branch-like arm. Another mom was dressed in a matching spandex outfit looking like she'd just come from the gym. The privileged mothers were just a reminder of how much of a loser I was. I hated them for that. All of them.

The bell finally rang and a few minutes later Rikki came bursting through the double doors with the rest of the kids. I knew something was up by the scowl plastered to his face. I leaned over and asked, "What's wrong Sweetie?"

"My feet are soaking Mom," he said, through clenched teeth.

"They let you play outside in the rain?"

"We have recess you know. Where else are we going to play?"

"But I, I... I'm, oh, I'm so sorry Rikki." I reached down to feel his shoe but he stepped away.

A surge of shame ran up the base of my neck. I was afraid the other moms might be judging me, so I kicked into crisis management mode, snapped my umbrella open and left. While Rikki and I took the Big Blue Bus, I was sure all the other kids were driving home in their luxury cars.

* * *

The following Saturday at our weekly house meeting everyone was running late. It was held in a converted garage with cold cement floors, second-hand couches, and foldout chairs. Ruth had arrived with the volunteers who would entertain the kids while we had our meeting. She always came with an assortment of donuts in hand. I was the first one to arrive.

"How ya doing Wendy?" she asked.

"I'm fine," I lied.

"Everything alright with your apartment?"

"Great."

I did not want to tell her how miserable I was living with Lara as I headed for the donuts and plopped down on the couch. A few minutes later, Leslie, a manic mother of two scruffy kids, came in.

"How's it going?" She sat next to me.

"Okay."

"I'm doing ninety in ninety." That meant she was going to a meeting every day for the next ninety days. Sounded as painful as eating glass to me.

Two women who didn't live at the house came to the meeting that morning. When it was time to get started, Ruth said, "Good morning ladies. How is everyone today?" There was the chorus of usual "fines" from all of us.

"I got a little surprise for you today." Ruth smiled. "I have two visitors with me today who are going to share their experience of when they went through the Women and Children Center. So, Becky, would you like to start?"

Becky was in her mid-thirties with hair that looked as wild as a lion's mane. As she talked of her dysfunctional childhood, in my mind I was comparing it to mine. Becky talked about how she used alcohol to fit in to a world and while I related to her, I would find any differences I could to separate me, being I was much more hard core.

After the meeting was over, I was about to leave when Becky stopped me. "How long have you been here?" she asked.

"A few months."

"How do you like it?"

"It's okay…" I wasn't convincing.

"Things get better if you just hang in there."

She was trying to encourage me but I had no experience of things ever getting better in my life so, I didn't believe her. All of the sudden, Rikki burst into the room carrying a tennis shoe in his hand. "Look Mom, the holes have gotten bigger."

My face turned red hot. I was mortified and felt all of the other mothers were judging me. "Rikki, I'm talking to someone right now." I glared at him with stern eyes.

Becky interrupted. "Does your son need a pair of shoes? I would be happy to buy him some."

Let me just say for the record, it was not normal for me to accept handouts from people, let alone from a complete stranger like Becky. It just didn't go with my finely tuned, tough girl persona, a by-product from living a defended life. But maybe because it was my son we were talking about, I paused only briefly before I relinquished my pride. "If you're sure you don't mind?"

"I would love to," Becky assured me.

For some reason I believed her. I knew she was looking for a way to help. And a few minutes later Rikki and I were piling into her car to make the short drive to Van's shoe store.

When we pulled up there was a sign in the window:

BUY ONE AND GET THE SECOND PAIR HALF OFF.

"With a sale like that I think you should really get two pairs," Becky said.

As I turned to look in the back seat, Rikki was all bouncy with his eyes wide and a big smile plastered on his face. While my heart was filled with joy for him I still felt a twinge of embarrassment to have a stranger buying him shoes, but I also felt like I didn't have a choice. And although I may not have been aware of it at the time, I had a belief system that convinced me it was a dog eat dog world. I had toughened up my insides to protect myself. But as much of a bad ass as I tried to be, it turned out I would have no defense against kindness and neither would my son.

Holy Shit

I thought about Jerry all the time. I wanted to see him but I didn't have a car or anyone to take me there. I wanted to send him money but barely had enough to live on. As we wrote letters back and forth I felt like our relationship was on the mend, considering he didn't want to talk to me when I first went to jail. I was thrilled when he told me in one of his letters that he might be getting out when he turned eighteen, which was only months away. I longed for the day to have my kids back together again.

Meanwhile, it was one of those rare and cherished nights when Lara was gone and Rikki and I could watch television in the living room without her voice bouncing off the walls. But first things first. Rikki needed to bathe. The bathroom was small and hard to maneuver in. It had an over-sized sink that jutted out from the wall. To get to the faucets I had to squeeze around the sink while extending my arm through the shower door to turn on the water. When I got the temperature the way he liked it, I yelled, "Your bath is ready."

"But Mom, I don't want to take a bath."

"You want to watch Fresh Prince of Bel Air, don't you?" I used his favorite shows as leverage.

A few minutes later, Rikki stood at the door with his pajamas tucked under his arm. At nine years old he was all lanky limbs but growing up fast.

"Just take a quick one."

"Alright Mom…." I left to give him some privacy.

I was about to light a cigarette, when Rikki yelled, "Mom come here! Hurry!"

Thinking he had fallen, I panicked. I rushed to the bathroom and flung the door open. Still dressed, he was pointing toward the tub.

I thought he was just trying to get out of taking a bath but I scooted passed him to have a look. My jaw must have come unhinged when I saw the small brown turd bobbing up and down in the water. "Oh shit." I said. And indeed, it was.

"I'm not taking a bath now. Jake shit in the tub. That's so gross."

"Alright, alright. Just put your pajamas on."

This wasn't my first encounter with shit while living there. Once I had sat down on the toilet and felt something squishy beneath me. I nearly jumped clear to the ceiling. When I looked down at the back of my thigh, there was brown sludge all over. When I told Lara that Jake had left it there, she seemed amused. "Oh, sorry," she shrugged. "I'll make sure to check next time."

The shit in the tub was the last straw. I had to find a way to get out of there. The next day I went over to see Ruth. Standing in her doorway I asked, "Can I talk to you?"

"Sure, Wendy come on in," Ruth said, smiling.

Plopping down on the couch, I crossed my arms across my chest.

"What's going on Wendy?"

"I'm having a hard time with my roommate."

I felt like I was snitching on Lara but for the first time I didn't care. I had to do something or I was going to leave. I explained how messy Lara was, how she was always on the phone and I told her about the shit in the bathtub. Ruth was calm and just nodded her head as she listened to me vent my stockpiled resentments.

After I presented a strong enough case, I asked, "Is there anywhere else we can live?"

Ruth sighed. "I'm afraid not."

My frustration quickened to despair. I lowered my chin to my chest.

"But I want you to try to hang in there for now," Ruth said, patting my knee. "You never know when something else might become available. Things can change quickly around here, but meanwhile, I'll have a little talk with Lara about cleaning up after herself."

"If you do that she'll know I said something and it will just make living with her worse."

Ruth's mind was working behind her eyes. "I think we are way overdue for an inspection at the center. I'll do a walk-through of everyone's apartment and that way she'll never suspect it was you. Meanwhile, why don't you pick up a television from the thrift store to put it in your bedroom?"

After that, I tried to have as little interaction with Lara as possible. Rikki and I stayed in our room mostly. If I moved through the house it was like I was crossing enemy territory. I had to find a way out of there.

*

It was six weeks later when Ruth called. "How would you like to have your own apartment by Rikki's school?"

"No way?"

This was completely unheard of because everyone shared an apartment with another mom.

"We just bought an eight-unit apartment complex in Santa Monica so you wouldn't have to take the bus anymore."

"When can I move in?"

"Come get the key so you can go take a look this afternoon and see if you're interested."

I was extremely interested and practically ran over to get the key. Ruth gave me the address and two keys and said, "I need to know as soon as possible because there are other people interested as well."

I got to Rikki's school early that day and when he came out I held out the key in the palm of my hand. "What's that?" he asked, raising an eyebrow.

"It's the key to our new apartment Ruth wants us to check out."

"Our own place?"

"Yeah. ...If we want it."

"We want it. We want it," he said, jumping up and down.

"Let's go look at it."

We walked briskly to 11th and Pico, which was a little less than a mile away. When we found the address, Rikki ran up the stairs in front of me. "Come on Mom. Hurry...."

The apartment was a two-story tan building with four units on each floor. It was eleven blocks from the beach. It had a narrow walkway in the front with a black iron hand rail leading upstairs. My heart raced with excitement as I opened the door with the key. I was hit with the smell of fresh paint. In the center of the living room were three small coffee tables stacked like a pyramid on top of each other. Rikki followed me into the kitchen where I opened cabinets doors and turned on the faucet to see if it worked. We explored the small modest bathroom together and finally the adjacent bedroom in the back. It definitely needed some work but I didn't care. It was ours and we wouldn't have to live with other people anymore. I looked at Rikki's brown eyes, flitting side-to-side as he tilted his head and asked, "Who's going to sleep in here?"

"You'll get your own bedroom now and I'll sleep in the living room."

He grabbed me around the waist and we both hugged each other tight. It felt like one dream had come true. All we ever wanted was to be on our own. The fact that I didn't run and things had actually worked out was an important lesson in my early recovery. One I would learn over and over again.

The Prodigal Son

We were given Carte Blanche at the Clare thrift store to furnish our apartment with whatever hand-me-downs we could find. I got a blue, fold-out futon for the living room and a small laminated table with a couple of mismatched chairs to put by the kitchen window overlooking Pico Boulevard. I got two televisions—one for Rikki's room so he could play Nintendo games whenever he wanted and one for the living room.

Rikki decorated his walls with posters of Michael Jordan. He had a twin bed, a dresser and a toy chest for all his GI Joe action figures. I loved being on our own. For one, I didn't have to ride back and forth on that bus anymore. I could watch whatever I wanted on television and for as long as I liked. For the first time, the future didn't feel so scary. For the first time, everything seemed like it might be okay after all.

What I didn't know then is that managing time was a learned skill. One I didn't have. What did I do with all my precious free time? I started to isolate. I ate ice cream. Took long naps. I started to clock my life by daytime programing: Days of Our Lives, reruns of I Love Lucy and The Andy Griffith Show.

The hours in the day would tick into night with me not accomplishing much of anything. I started feeling depressed. It was the same darkness that consumed me as a kid. After all, I was a deeply flawed human being and destined to live out the rest of my life just getting by.

One day I was laying around when I heard a knock on the door. I startled. Human interactions were difficult and I wasn't expecting anyone. I knew Rikki was still in school because Oprah Winfrey was still on. Maybe it was someone from Clare

Foundation coming over to make sure I wasn't shooting-up drugs or having orgies in my living room.

I opened the door just a crack to make sure it wasn't a rapist.

"Jerry, oh my God!" I pulled the door open and threw my arms around my eldest son who was six feet of rock-hard muscle. His hair was buzzed close to his scalp and he was wearing over-sized, khaki shorts and a white sling-shot t-shirt.

"Hi Mom." His brow was furrowed, his brown eyes intense. His expression reminded me just how uncomfortable I could be on any given day.

"You got out? Oh my God." I waved him in. "When were you released?"

"A couple weeks ago."

"Why didn't you call?"

"I don't know," he said, defensively. "I just wanted to surprise you I guess."

"Well it's a good surprised alright…" I hugged him again.

"Where's Rikki?" he asked.

"School. He should be home pretty soon." The thought of finally having my boys back together pushed back the darkness I had been feeling moments before. "He's going to be so happy to see you."

I held his wrist to examine an intricate tattoo of a castle that wrapped around his right bicep. "Is that new?"

"Yeah… a homie did it for me while I was locked up."

I nodded.

Jerry scanned the room. "So, when did you move in here?"

"Just recently got it though an organization that helps people get clean and sober."

"So, you're actually clean now?" He raised an eyebrow suspiciously.

"Well. I'm trying but it's not easy."

"Yeah. I bet."

Paranoid he might have heard about my recent relapse from his Dad, I changed the subject. "I've missed you Jerry. I thought about you every day in jail."

"I'm sorry I didn't write back. There just wasn't much to say."

"Don't worry. I get it." I laid an arm around his massive shoulder. "How was it in there?"

"It was okay. I had a few homies looking out for me."

"Did anyone mess with you?"

"Look at me Mom." He flexed his tattooed arm. "You think anyone would mess with me?"

"No, I guess not." I shook my head.

"You got an extra smoke?"

I leaned over to pick up the pack of cigarettes on the coffee table and tapped one out for him. Just then Rikki opened the front door and froze. His jaw came unhinged.

In true athletic form, Rikki leaped into his brother's arms, wrapping his lanky legs around the back of Jerry's thick calves.

"Holy shit bro!" Jerry laughed. "You've gotten so big."

"You're the one who's gotten big, Dee." Rikki still used the nickname that he had given his older brother when he was learning to talk. "You must have eaten a lot in there."

"Not much else to do." Jerry gently set his brother back down.

"You want to play the new Nintendo game, Bases Loaded?"

"Sure," Jerry shrugged

"I bet I can beat you at it." Rikki pulled his big brother by the arm.

"We'll just have to see about that." They both disappeared into the bedroom.

A quiet and deep relief expanded across my chest. This was all I thought about in the county jail. My boys. Me and my sweet boys back together again. I started thinking maybe Jerry could stay with us for a while? I knew the rules at Clare wouldn't allow it because he was eighteen, but I could always say he was just visiting me. That was allowed. And since supervision was minimal, if Jerry kept a low profile no one would even know he was there. I had visions of my boys playing basketball together. I imagined Jerry could get a job and I could make him dinner when he got home from work. I was determined to make up for all the years of being an addict.

Later that night I was in heaven as we watched Three's Company and ate pepperoni pizza. Eventually Rikki's eyes were at half-mast and his chin started falling to his chest. I made him go to his own bed as I laid out extra blankets and a comforter with a pillow on the living room floor for Jerry.

"I hope this is okay."

"Yeah, Mom. I've been sleeping on hard ass bunks. It'll be fine." Jerry lay down and pulled the covers up over him.

"I'm so happy that you're here with us." I turned off the lights.

"Yeah me too, Mom."

The next morning Jerry was rolled up in blankets like a human burrito. He snored so loud it sounded like the pipes of a Harley Davidson. We all quietly stepped over him as Rikki got ready for school.

He finally woke around noon. "Good morning Jerry," I said all perky-like.

"Morning…" he grumbled.

After he went to the bathroom, he headed for the kitchen to pour himself a bowl of cereal. He was on his second bowl when I made the mistake of saying something. "Can you go a little easy on the cereal? I don't have enough to last the week."

"Why do you always do that to me?" he snapped.

"Do what?"

"Ration food."

I thought it was self-preservation since I was on welfare, I had to make ends meet. Didn't I? But I didn't know I had my father's voice echoing inside my brain. My dad had lost everything due to his alcoholism. We transitioned from luxury as kids to him going completely bankrupt when we were teenagers. So, I went from being a privileged white girl to rationing the food. Now I was imprinting the same message of scarcity onto my own kids, only I didn't know it at the time.

I thought it best to stop helicoptering around Jerry while he ate and retreated to the living room. My fantasies of being one happy family were replaced with thoughts of 'Jerry must hate me.' And who could really blame him if he did?

Jerry stayed a few days until he said he had to go.

"Where are you heading?" I asked.

"To Lomita." That was where we used to live. I knew he'd probably get in trouble down there.

"You sure that's such a good idea?"

"Yeah Mom. Why not?"

"It's just don't want you to go back to jail is all."

"I need to see the homies, Mom," he said, before he left.

Jerry wouldn't listen to me just like I never listened to my dad. Just like my father had been powerless over what I did, I couldn't stop my son from getting high. Clearly, there was a heap of karmic debt that was overdue.

Circling The Drain

I hadn't heard from Jerry for several weeks and I was worried sick. These were the days before cell phones. I was left to wonder, what the hell was he doing out there? What if he got arrested or worse, overdosed on heroin or something. Every time the phone rang I would jump. I thought something bad was going to happen and knew it would be all my fault. But maybe Jerry never had a chance to begin with considering all the generations stacked upon generations, of alcoholism and mental illness running through our blood. What had I been thinking having kids?

There was a part of me that wanted to join him. At least if I were able to get high I could escape my thoughts that hit me over the head like a hammer. I wouldn't go off the deep end this time. Besides drugs had been the problem. Not alcohol. And a bottle of chilled wine would take the edge off. I could drink it while Rikki was at school and no one would ever know.

Six weeks later a much thinner version of Jerry showed up at my door. His skin had a grayish pallor to it and there were dark raccoon circles under his eyes. "Is everything alright?" I asked as I let him in.

"What do you mean?" he snapped.

"Well it looks like you've lost some weight…."

He interrupted, "So what… I needed to lose some weight."

Our relationship was loaded and hard to navigate. I couldn't just come out and ask him if he was doing drugs. Besides, I would feel like a hypocrite if I did.

Jerry stayed again, obviously recuperating from all the drugs he had been doing. He slept in every day. Eventually, he'd wake up and make himself something to eat. It felt like I was walking on egg-shells.

After a week of this, I grew tired of Jerry sleeping in and having to be quiet in my own house. I nudged his shoulder to wake him up. "Can you go sleep in Rikki's room? He's at school."

He let out a long, exasperated sigh.

"Jerry please...."

"All right Mom!" Throwing back the blankets he pushed himself up.

I thought I heard him say, "bitch" and my defenses flipped up. "What did you say?"

Our tempers quickly escalated. As we went back and forth, he rattled off a long list of things he was angry with me about.

"It's your fault my life is like it is."

"Don't blame me for your life!"

"Well, if you weren't a drug addict I would have had more of a chance."

Yelling and blaming each other instead of addressing the loads of hurt we felt was easier than seeking therapeutic support. If he pointed at events where I had let him down I pointed back.

"Trying to shoot dad was fucking stupid."

"You weren't even there so you don't know what happened."

"Whose mother does that anyway?"

"Who talks to their mother the way you do with me?"

"That's because you ruined my life."

This would go on until Jerry finally grabbed his jacket and slammed the door behind him. After he left, I stood there. My hands were shaking. White noise flooded my brain. I rushed to the bathroom to splash water on my face. I saw my reflection in the mirror and cringed. I was a bad person. A bad mother who'd destroyed her children's lives and getting sober wasn't going to change any of that.

If only I could splash water on my insides where all the real dirt resided.

A tsunami of self-hatred flooded me. I wanted some relief but what could possibly make me feel better? I had nothing in the house to anesthetize my pain. I lit a cigarette and paced back and forth in the living room. My stomach felt all tied up in knots.

A few minutes later I was headed down Pico Boulevard to the corner liquor store. I had to pass CLARE Foundation on the way. Ruth had recently been promoted to executive director and her offices were just two blocks away now. For some reason, instead of getting something to drink, I turned right to go talk to Ruth.

I stood at the door just like I did that first day. "Do you have a minute?" I asked.

"Oh. Hi Wendy. Yes, of course." She waved me in.

I sat down in one of the chairs afraid to incriminate myself so I stared at the floor.

"What's going on?" Ruth asked.

I paused then said, "My older son, Jerry... he got out of juvenile hall."

I told her almost everything but left out the part about him probably using drugs.

"Jerry blames me for everything that's wrong in his life."

Ruth nodded. "My boys did the same thing with me when I first got sober."

"What did you do?"

"I stopped engaging with them."

"What does that mean exactly?"

"I stopped defending myself."

"But Jerry says horrible things and I feel like I have to defend myself."

"If you stop doing the dance he won't have anyone to dance with."

Ruth was Yoda-wise. I let out an exasperated sigh and nodded my head.

"Okay I will give it a try."

Boundaries

When Jerry showed up two weeks later it was obvious he was doing drugs. His cheeks were sunken in and his eyes looked like two vacant pools. Seeing him like that broke my heart. I felt like if he kept it up, his pilot light would go out. When he stayed over again nothing had changed. He slept in every day, he'd wake up grumpy and take the phone to the bathroom to call his friends. I felt like I had to be hyper vigilant about everything I said because he seemed so angry with me.

One day I was washing dishes when he poured himself a second bowl of cereal. "Jerry please go easy on that. I don't have any money to get more."

The air seemed to get sucked out of the room. I shifted nervously. It felt like I had made a big mistake. He slammed down the spoon on the table and glared at me.

"Why don't you ever do that to Rikki?"

"I tell Rikki all the time."

He stood up. "No, you don't. And besides if you weren't such a bad mom I might not be in this fucking situation."

His words felt like tiny arrows landing between my shoulder blades. I bit down on my molars trying to refrain from my usual defensive mode. *Don't engage. Don't engage*, I chanted inside my head. As I continued to wash the same plate in circular motions, he yelled at me from behind. There was an icy chill running up the back of my neck.

"You were never there for me. All my friends had parents who cared... "

His words hurt but I kept hearing Ruth's voice echoing inside my brain. 'Don't do the dance with him.'

Instead I said the Serenity Prayer. "Grant me the serenity to accept the things I cannot change, the courage to change the things I can. And the wisdom to know the difference."

My face turned hot. I took a deep breath and turned around to face him. He was shifting on the balls of his feet. My Playtex gloves dripped water on the floor and with a calm voice that I didn't recognize, I said, "The woman you're talking about doesn't live here anymore." I pointed a sudsy finger to my chest.

My words stopped him mid-breath. Jerry was ready for a fight but I had thrown a curve ball. His chest heaved with anger but he didn't know what to say. I had changed the script. Flustered, he grunted something under his breath and went into the bathroom. My heart was racing until a few minutes later he took his things and left.

I peeled off my Playtex gloves and plopped down on the living room couch. My whole body was trembling. Even though I was deeply shaken, I knew something had shifted in me. I'd like to say I had learned once and for all how to set boundaries, but that wasn't the case. Yet just for that one day, I hadn't done the dance.

Mother's Day

It was late on Mother's Day. Rikki was asleep in his room while Janet, a woman I met at one of those meetings I hated, had come over to watch TV. Janet was short, high energy and a little bit of a geek—definitely not someone I'd typically hang out with. We were both slumped down on the couch watching the apocalyptic horror of Stephen King's The Stand. When the phone rang. I knew it had to be Jerry because who else would be calling so late? I looked at Janet who gave me a reassuring nod.

I got up, let out a sigh before I picked up the receiver. "Hello?"

"Hey Mom, I'm coming over."

I took a deep breath. "I'm sorry, Jerry, you can't come here unless you are interested in getting some help." As soon as I said it I wanted to suck the words back into my lungs.

"Well fuck you then!" He slammed down the phone.

It felt like I was sucker punched in the gut. I walked back in a daze. "Are you okay?" Janet asked.

"No, no… I'm not okay." Grabbing a cigarette, I lit up and plopped back down on the couch and went silent. For fuck sake, it was Mother's Day. I should have just let him come and stay with us. I am his mom after all.

All of a sudden, I heard, POW, POW, POW, POW!

"What was that?" Janet exclaimed.

"It sounded like a gun."

I jumped up and peered out the mini-blinds. I was stunned when I saw a body lying in the crosswalk on the street below.

"Oh my God! Someone's been shot!"

As a self-centered addict, I was conditioned not to get involved in other people's business, and that went double if cops were likely to show. But maybe because it was Mother's Day or because my son had just hung up on me, or maybe because I was newly sober, I did something completely out of character. I rushed out the front door, down the stairs and across the street.

The victim was Latino and around nineteen years old. Jerry's age. He was face down, wearing a thick black and white Pendleton, with one arm raised over his head, the other along his side. I didn't see any blood so I dropped down on my knees to get a better look. I leaned over and there was a long strand of saliva hanging like a single guitar string from the corner of his mouth. A throb of panic rippled through me.

What the hell am I supposed to do now? I don't even know CPR.

I looked up at my neighbors gathered in small, hushed groups on the sidewalk. And as if reading my mind, a woman yelled, "I called 911. They're on the way."

I leaned over and whispered, "Please hang in there," while gently stroking his back.

A rattle sounding like a marble rolling over corrugated steel came from deep inside his lungs. Fear seized me. A part of me wanted to run but it felt like an invisible curtain had come down around us. It was just me and him. Time slowed to a crawl. I felt the grit of cement pressing beneath my knees. The air held the hint of red tide from the ocean several blocks away. The street lamps cast an eerie glow over everything. I was afraid he wouldn't make it.

Please don't die, please don't die, please don't die, I chanted inside my head.

It seemed to take forever, but finally, I heard sirens wailing in the distance.

"They're coming. They're almost here... " I gently rubbed his back again. "Hang in there. They're going to help you."

Within minutes, a dozen patrol cars were on the scene. And for the first time in my life I was relieved to see so many cops. One of them pushed the crowd back while he started to secure the intersection with yellow tape. I looked back to the kid when a young officer stood over me.

"Are you his mother?" he gently asked.

"No, no, I'm not his mother. I live up there." I pointed to my apartment building.

"Then you need to get behind the line, lady." His tone instantly changed.

I didn't want to leave that boy. I wanted to stay with him. He needed me. But even under those circumstances, I knew it was pointless to argue with cops. The officer helped me up by the back of my arm and escorted me to where the other onlookers stood behind the yellow tape.

A round woman with spongy pink curlers shuffled over. "What do you think happened?"

"He's been shot," I said, stating the obvious.

"Who could do such a thing?" One curler came loose as she shook her head.

I knew it could have been anything from a drug deal gone bad to a random drive-by.

Finally, the ambulance arrived. Two paramedics rushed over to the boy, flipped him over and appeared to be listening to his heart. I was glad to see they weren't wasting any time as they loaded him onto the stretcher. However, just as they were about to load him into the ambulance, they stopped. I craned my neck as one of the paramedics reached for what I now know was a defibrillator. They ripped open his shirt and set-up the pads on his chest. His whole torso arched as they sent a jolt of electricity to his failing heart.

Please don't die, please don't die please don't die.

Two minutes later the ambulance was taking off with lights flashing, sirens blaring straight up Pico Boulevard. My insides were shaking with the adrenaline as a cop yelled, "Alright everyone, the show is over now. Unless you actually saw something tonight, you can all go home now."

I needed a fucking cigarette. Bad. I turned around and headed back across the street and up the stairs. Janet met me at the top, "Are you okay?"

I walked past her and went directly for the pack of smokes on the coffee table. My hands shook as I struck the match. Fear gripped me. "It's a sign something bad is going to happen... I... should have never told Jerry he couldn't come here."

"Oh honey...he'll be alright."

I smoked that cigarette and lit up another. My head was spinning. When Janet tried to console me again, I was annoyed. After all, she didn't have kids so how could she know?

"Look, I'm tired. I want to go to bed."

She studied me for a moment and finally said, "Okay but if you need anything please don't hesitate to call me..."

"Of course."

I think we both knew I never would.

After she left, it felt like my brain was eating itself alive. Why the hell did I tell Jerry that? I wished I could find him. But this was before cell phones and I didn't know where he was. Man, I wanted a fucking drink. No one would even know if I went to the liquor store and got something. And after what I just went through, who could blame me?

What stopped me in the end? I didn't want to pass those cops who were scanning the crime scene and I had a small boy asleep in the other room. Fuck! My anxiety was off the charts. Sleep was my only possible option to find an escape.

I didn't want to be alone so I grabbed my bedding and headed for Rikki's room. After I picked up the GI Joe figures, I spread the blankets on the floor. I could smell the pre-adolescent musk hanging in the air. I paused briefly to watch the gentle rise and fall of Rikki's chest. At least I knew where one of my boys was.

Please Jerry be safe out there. Please be safe. Please be safe.

As I lay down, my thoughts came at me like the rat-a-tat-tat of an AK47. How would I ever know what happened to that boy? Did his mother know? Oh my God. His poor mother. Maybe it was a sign that something bad was going to happen to Jerry? Why the fuck did I tell him he couldn't come over? I felt all the classic signs of a panic attack coming on. The tightness in my chest. The shortness of breath. The walls squeezing in on me. I started to hyperventilate. And then something happened. Something I still find hard to explain.

A presence entered the room through the ceiling in the form of a soft, shimmering, white light. Cascading downward it poured itself into my heart and spread out across my chest. The white noise in my brain completely shut off. In an instant, I went from heightened anxiety to an absolute state of peace. There was silence. Somehow, I knew 'everything was alright'. Always had been alright, and always would be alright. It was a feeling I had never had before. Eventually the light slipped away. 'What was that?' If it was God it was clearly not the one I grew up with. That light felt like a pure energy source that reached across some other worldly realms. I didn't know it yet, but I would never be the same.

Surrender To Win

When I woke up the next morning my thoughts swirled in. On one level, I knew the peace I experienced the night before was real. In fact, it was more real than anything I'd ever felt before, however, my mind was starting to second-guess itself. Did that really happen or was it just my imagination? Maybe I was just dreaming?

Rikki was still asleep so I pushed myself up and went into living room to light a cigarette. I peeked out of the mini-blinds and it was all business as usual down on the street. No sign of the police. No yellow crime tape cordoning off the intersection anymore. People were on their way to work, the wheels of cars and buses rolling over the place where that poor boy had lain the night before. I wondered about that poor boy. Was he alive? Was he laying in some hospital on life support somewhere? I asked everyone in the building if they knew anything. But no one did.

It wasn't until later that morning when Rikki was at school that I heard a soft knock. When I opened the door there was a neighbor with a somber look on her face.

"The boy didn't make it."

"How do you know?"

"My friend is a dispatcher at the Santa Monica Police Department and she told me he died at the hospital last night."

After she had gone I felt such an overwhelming sense of sorrow. Not only for him, but his mother as well. I wanted to find her and tell her how her son had not been alone. But I never would. I wondered if it was perhaps that boy's spirit who came to me the night before. Did he want to thank me for staying by his side? Maybe that was it? The thought caused an ache so profound to rise up from deep inside me. The pain I felt seemed oddly disproportionate for a complete stranger.

Images of the boy's face pressed against the cement kept appearing in my head. I thought about Jerry. I wanted him to call me so I could tell him to please come over. I wanted to protect him from the drugs, the drive-bys and all the other dangers in life.

My brain felt like it was eating itself alive. I decided to get out of the house so I walked to the local market. I was crossing the parking lot in a daze when I heard someone call my name. My head turned back and forth trying to figure out where the voice was coming from. "Wendy, over here!" it said again.

My gaze landed on Sarah, a girl I had seen at meetings. We hardly ever talked and I found it odd she even remembered my name. Sarah was blond, with flawless skin and perfectly arched eyebrows. I walked over to her car.

"How's it going, girl?" Sarah said, smiling.

"Not good...."

"What's wrong?" She moved a bit closer.

"I saw a boy get shot in front of my apartment last night."

"Oh my God! You're kidding?" Her hand shot up to her mouth. "That's terrible."

I gave her the Reader's Digest version.

"There's a noon women's meeting in a few minutes. "We should go," she said.

"But I need to get groceries."

"I'll bring you back after," she leaned over and released the lock of the passenger door on her shiny BMW.

For some reason I didn't argue, and crawled into the front seat. Ten minutes later Sarah was leading me by the arm to the front row of a meeting held in a church.

The speaker was a conservative woman in her sixties. And while her mouth was moving, I didn't hear a thing. I was too busy trying to hold back a tsunami of grief that was rising up in my chest. My throat clenched tight. I was keeping it back with sheer will power. *Don't cry, don't cry, don't you dare fucking cry.*

When the speaker was done, the meeting was opened up for anyone else who wanted to share. Sarah leaned over and gave me a nudge. "Raise your hand," she said.

My arm shot straight up as if pulled by an invisible string. "A boy was shot in front of me last night. And I'm worried the same thing could happen to my son."

For the first time, I didn't care what anybody thought about me. I sobbed. And not in some dainty way either. There was snot and tears. I cried for all the times I hadn't cried before. I cried for that boy. I cried for my own boys and I even cried for me. Most of the women in that room were nothing like me but I didn't care. When I finished sobbing a dozen white tissues were passed in my direction like tiny white flags of surrender. I was done. I had finally let go. I let go of the idea that I had to hold my shit together. I let go of the idea that being strong was the ability to tuck my feelings away so no one else would ever know who I was. I let go of doing my life alone. I learned that being vulnerable gave me a different kind of strength. And that's a lesson I am still learning today.

The Path Gets Narrower

When you get sober, the path gets narrower or that was certainly the case with me. It meant I could find fewer things that I could reach for to comfort myself. Some addicts use retail therapy as a means of instant gratification but I was broke most of the time, so that didn't work. Others engage in random sex to get validation. I'm sure if I didn't have a young boy sleeping in the other room I would have been doing the same thing as well.

Instead, I stole things. Small things, mostly. Like shampoo, mascara and lipstick or anything that could fit inside my purse. Besides the obvious payoff of saving money, I loved the adrenaline rush I got when getting away with something. There is a lot of excitement that goes with being a drug addict and that was, for the most part, gone. When I stole, adrenaline would pump through my blood stream. It was another way for me to get high.

I first time I stole was in the mid-seventies when I got strung out on heroin. I was twenty-two and needed a way to support my hefty drug habit. When I asked Sammy, a sucked-up-dope-fiend with greasy black hair about it, he said, "Well, I figure you can either sell your body or boost meat." He itched his nose with the back of his hand.

"But why meat?"

"Because housewives pay top dollar for it."

"They don't care if it's stolen?"

"We don't discuss how I got the meat. All I know is a wife loves a deal, especially if it saves them the time of cutting out coupons from the Sunday Times. I'm sort of like a modern-day Robin Hood, if you think about it." Sammy winked.

Not long after that I found myself pushing a shopping cart wearing a big jacket, baggy jeans and a leather belt. I headed for the butcher's section where I found rows of bulging pink meat, sealed in saran wrap inside the open freezer. When no one was around I dropped meat in my cart and covered it up with the cereal boxes I had gotten beforehand.

When I had enough I rolled my cart down an aisle and stopped midway and loosened my belt. I would stuff steaks in the waistband until I looked like a suicide bomber about to blow the place up with meat. But that was years ago.

I was sober now and you'd think I'd know better than to shoplift. But no. Not me. My mind could rationalize and justify any sketchy behavior that served my selfish needs. I told myself I was a single mom and couldn't afford things that other people could afford. Didn't I deserve the necessities everyone else had? Besides, it wasn't like I was stealing meat.

But stealing was different sober, because I was starting to develop a conscience. I had been doing it off and on since I got out of jail. But lately it seemed that whenever I stole, I'd feel a tug of guilt. These new, strange feelings were as foreign to me as paying my taxes had been.

One day while Rikki was at school, I was at one of my favorite stores with a plan just to get a few things. I grabbed a handheld basket and draped it over my forearm. I slipped a cherry flavored lip gloss inside my purse. I felt a constriction in my chest. I inhaled. My ribs contracted. My heart was pumping hard. I imagine it exploding inside my chest and me dying on the spot. Why the hell was I so scared all of a sudden? I pushed through these uncomfortable feelings and crouched down, pretending to look at merchandise on the bottom shelf. With my eyes darting back and forth, I slipped a bottle of hair conditioner inside my purse. When I got back up too fast I got dizzy. I told myself not to pass out because if I did someone would be forced to rifle through my purse and they'd find more than my identification. I wanted to make a mad dash for it. I willed my feet to move, one step at a time. Slowly, and steadily, being careful not to bring any undue attention to myself. The trick to stealing was to stay cool. I was just about to turn the corner when a clerk with thick black eye-liner popped up out of nowhere. "Can I help you with something?"

"Ah, no. I'm just browsing around, but thanks."

"Let me know if you need any help." The sales girl turned and marched away on her pumps.

Shit! Fuck! Did I hear a hint of suspicion in her voice or was I just being paranoid? What the hell should I do? I pretended to study a box of hair color as adrenaline pumped through my veins. Everything in me was on high alert. Every color brighter, every noise louder. I used to push through the fear, but for the first time, I was weighing my options. If I walked out the door the clerk might be waiting for me, or worse, the police. I would obviously go to jail. Since I had a record, I could be charged with 'petty with a prior,' which would bump it up to a felony. What would Rikki do if I went to jail again? It would clearly break his heart. I made sure no one was around when I put the items back on the shelf.

I don't know when, but eventually I learned that relapse starts long before you actually pick up that first drink. While I was looking for it to come in through the front door, it was trying to sneak in the back door. The disease is so baffling it seems to know each addict's vulnerability. My vulnerability was the deep yearning to have what everyone else seemed to have. But I was not only risking my freedom for a tube of lip gloss, I would also hurt everybody who had started believing in me. So instead of despairing about what was lacking in my life, I had to learn to appreciate the things I did have. I wasn't in jail any more. I had enough money to eat. I was no longer killing myself with drugs and alcohol. When I looked hard enough there was plenty to be grateful for.

Self-Supporting

I was thrilled to get my first job. As soon as Rikki got home from school with a basketball tucked under his arm, I gave him the good news. "Guess what, Becky gave me a job at the doctor's office she works at."

"Does that mean I can buy some new sneakers?"

"It's a part time job Rikki. I doubt that we can buy any designer shoes."

"Everybody else has them at school."

"I can't keep up with those kids and besides there is more to life than having the latest Air Jordans."

We were on the cusp of a massive generational gap and I didn't understand his budding obsession with sneakers.

Monday morning, I felt like I was a real grown up when I arrived early to show my new employers how dedicated I would be. Becky was the office manager, she gave me a tour showing me each of the exam rooms and the three doctors' offices that wrapped around in an L shape. When we were coming back up the hall we ran into one of doctors, a wiry, short man with a receding hairline.

"Dr. Frankel, this is Wendy. She will be filing charts for us from now on."

"Nice to meet you Wendy." He held out his hand.

My head dropped. "Nice to meet you." My voice was soft.

I will never forget the way Dr. Frankel bent down and tilted his face practically forcing me to make direct eye contact with him. I smiled awkwardly. My skin felt all prickly. I probably would have run out the back door if I didn't need the job so much. It seemed that anyone with an education or status could push my 'less than' button. Back then I had an internal measuring stick. I came up short with any individual that had letters behind their name. Dr. Frankel saw through my thin veneer and gazed right into my low self-esteem. As a result, I was humiliated. When I walked away, I made a mental note to give the doctor a wide birth.

My job was simple. All I had to do was file medical charts in alphabetical order and labs under the correct tab. Easy. I knew the alphabet, so I figured I'd be able to manage that. But after a month at my new job, Becky called me into her office. "Dr. Frankel found one of his patient's chart in the wrong place." Her tone was like a parent scolding a child.

I felt the familiar tug of shame at the base of my neck. "Oh. I'm sorry. I'll be more careful next time."

"Please do Wendy. He's a busy man and doesn't want to be wasting time looking for medical charts."

"Um, okay. I'm sorry. I'm sorry." I bit on my lower lip.

A more well-adjusted individual might have interpreted this feedback as constructive criticism, but not me. I instantly started beating myself up.

You're so stupid Wendy. You can't even put the charts in the right place. Maybe you should stay on welfare.

The moment my brain's critic clicked on I was no longer present. I looked like I was doing my job, but I wasn't paying attention anymore. As a result, the next day I found a trail of misfiled charts that were like bread crumbs leading back to the moment I started my self-deprecating spin. The way I talked to myself, I would never talk to anyone else. My internal voices were brutal and cruel. It was clear my internal dialogue needed to change. But how?

I needed a kinder, gentler voice. One that was encouraging, supportive and kind. Perhaps, one that talked to me like a loving mother might have.

The next time Becky called me into her office and scolded me for misfiling charts I was ready for her. "Okay. I'm sorry, I will be more careful."

When I left her office, I chiseled down through the pile of charts. I tried a different approach. While the old voices were still clamoring to be heard, I coached myself with new dialogue, *'You're a human being and everybody makes mistakes. No big deal. You'll pay better attention from here on out.'* As I slipped each chart into their proper alphabetic slot, I forced myself to pay attention. I started saying the letters out loud to make sure they registered inside my brain.

As an escape artist, I had lost decades of my life on drugs only to pop-out on the other side with very few life skills on board. In order not to be overwhelmed, I had to do that job just like I did my sobriety, one chart at a time.

An Apple Falls in My Lap

I hadn't heard from Jerry for several months. One day the phone rang, and when I picked it up I heard the same familiar tinny recording that I heard when I was in jail coming from the other end. "This is a collect call originating from a Los Angeles County Correctional Facility. Do you wish to accept charges from Jerry Mendias?" My stomach clenched. I punched the key hard, indicating that hell yeah, I wanted to accept the charges.

"Mom?"

"Jerry what's going on?"

"I'm in county jail, Mom."

"Why, what, happened?"

"Oh Mom, I did something really bad."

I pressed my hand against the wall for support. My breath felt like it was cut off.

"I, I, I was at a party and some crazy guy pulled a knife on me. We got in a fight and I somehow managed to get the knife and I was so loaded...I, I, I stabbed him with it." He sounded like he was crying.

"Is, is... the guy alright?"

"Yeah, yeah, thank God, he's okay. I was in a blackout Mom. I can only remember parts of what happened."

"How much is your bail?" I gripped the phone cord.

A long release of air. ".... fifty thousand."

"God, I wish I could get you out." We both knew that was impossible.

He paused. "I really feel horrible for what I did."

I nodded. "Believe me, I know what that's like. I felt horrible too after I shot Cat."

"Really? You did?" He sounded surprised.

"Oh yeah. I was devastated. Not only about losing your father, but hurting someone."

"Mom, I'm so sorry I was such an asshole to you."

"I'm sorry too Jerry. I've been an asshole for a very long time."

I could hear him crying. Jerry had always been an emotional tough guy.

"I love you, Mom."

"I love you too, son."

After we hung up, I wiped my face with the palms of my hands. I was frightened for Jerry because now he was in adult jail, not juvenile hall. I prayed over and over again that he would be safe in there.

The fact that he had been arrested for assault with a deadly weapon, the same charge I had been arrested for was mind-blowing. I thought, clearly the sins of the mother had been passed down to the son. Had I gotten sober too late to make a difference for my son? Were the effects of my life-style imprinted in his psyche? How could I ever make it up to him?

Breaking the Cycle

A few weeks had gone by when I opened the front door and found Max standing there with his clothes shabby and loose. He had dark plum circles under both his eyes. Like they used to say in jail, he was 'tore up from the floor up.'

"Oh, hey Max. I wasn't expecting you."

"Oh sorry. I just thought I'd stop by to see Rikki."

"Come on in. He should be home from school any minute."

Max gave me a hug that seemed to linger a couple of seconds too long before sitting down in a chair. I sat across from him on the couch.

"You heard about Jerry?" he asked.

"Yeah. He called me."

"It fucking sucks."

I nodded my head. "I'm really worried about him."

"He's a tough kid. He'll be alright."

"But jail is a lot different than juvenile hall."

"Believe me, that boy can take care of himself."

He changed the subject. "You're looking mighty fit these days," Max said, with a wink. "Whatever you're doing is working." Max tilted his head sideways with a half-smile.

He was flirting again, only I felt nothing for him anymore. He pushed himself up and reached deep in the front pocket of his jeans. "I brought you a little something."

I felt a sudden rush of anxiety made up of equal parts, desire and unease. I knew what was coming before I laid eyes on the folded paper stretched out in the palm of Max's hand. Kryptonite. My heart pounded against my chest. I had never turned down drugs before. They had always been my escape hatch. There was a moment, a brief millisecond, where I could have snatched it from his hand, but instead I paused, took a breath and said, "I'm not getting high anymore."

"But I, I, I brought it. I thought…"

"I really like being sober, Max."

Max knew me as a girl who couldn't take a sober breath. And believe me, I was just as surprised as him.

"Wow. You really have changed, haven't you?"

"Yes. I want more out of life than being a hopeless drug addict."

I could see his mind working behind his eyes as he studied me.

"So, what do you like about it so much?" Max slipped the drugs back in his pocket and sat back down.

"Well, for one, I don't wake up with regret every day."

His glassy brown eyes stared. "I just never thought you'd ever be able to stop."

"I never thought I could either, so I never bothered to try. I thought being an addict is the cards I had been dealt and I had no choice but to play the hand. And Max…" I let out a long sigh. "I just wanted to tell you how sorry I am for everything."

His eyes narrowed. "For what?"

"Well, for one thing, chasing you down with a gun that night."

"Oh, that." He smiled. "Well yeah, you should apologize for that."

"No. Really, I could have handled it a whole lot better."

The corner of his mouth curled up. "I'll never forget how you had that gun holster and blue bandanna wrapped around your forehead."

"What? I was not wearing a bandanna or holster." I laughed out loud.

"You were totally Rambo'd-out in full combat regalia."

I cracked up. "You were definitely seeing things because I was not…"

And while Max still swears that's the way I was dressed, it just goes to show that memories are not always a perfect representation of what actually happened. And since neither of us have photographs or a movie of that night, I guess we'll never know. On the other hand, it felt so good to be laughing about it. I never in my wildest dreams thought that would be possible. Ever.

The Scene of the Crime

Feeling like the proverbial criminal returning to the scene of the crime, I climbed the long steps to the Torrance Courthouse. It had been six weeks since Jerry got arrested and he was scheduled to appear in court. I was nervous about the possibility of being recognized by some cop who knew me back when, or worse, I'd run into some sketchy tweaker from the old hood.

My heart raced as I pushed the glass doors open with my shoulder and stepped inside. Attorneys dressed in three-piece suits who carry briefcases pushed their way onto the elevators. Uniformed cops huddled together in the hallway, craning their necks for any suspicious characters. Obviously, there were quite a few of those around. Defendants, ranging from maybe a student who stole mascara, to a gangbanger facing multiple drug charges, made the courthouse look like a three-ring circus.

Powering up mentally, I lowered my head, clutched my purse to my ribs like a football player, and weaved my way through the crowd. I may have looked like a wide-receiver, but I was merely trying to make it to the far wall. When I got there, I squeezed sideways to scan the list of names of defendants appearing in court that day. My eyes went up and down until I landed on Jerry's full name. I was stunned he was appearing in front of a judge I had been in front of before.

It was back when I was a twenty-two-year-old junkie that I first encountered the Honorable Judge Aranda. That was when I was stealing meat, but as an innovative junkie, I carried a fake I.D on me at all times. And wouldn't you know it, over the course of a year, I got arrested three times under three different aliases. Being that petty theft was a misdemeanor, I would be taken to the substation, booked, cited and told I needed to show up for my court appearance before I was released. Seeing how it was a fake ID, I never would go to court because I figured I was a fictitious character. However, with modern technology rolling along such as it was, when I got arrested again, my fingerprints were put into a new data base and warrants started popping up like I'd hit the petty-theft lottery or something.

For three consecutive days in a row I appeared in front of Judge Aranda under different names. On the third day, Aranda, who seemed thoroughly annoyed, glared at me over his rectangular glasses and said, "Well, who do we have the honor of appearing before us today?"

Of course, the jig was up, so I gave my real name and was sentenced to nine months for all three charges. I made a mental note back then to avoid Judge Aranda's courtroom no matter what. But there I was, squeezing myself into the elevator with all the attorneys, voluntarily making my way to his courtroom for the sake of my eldest son

As I stood in front of the double doors, I took a deep breath and stepped inside. There was a bailiff with a body that looked as firm as steel-belted radials. I stood obediently behind the divider until he looked up from his paperwork.

"How can I help you?" He stood up and walked toward me.

"I'd like to talk to my son's attorney if I could."

"What's your son's name?"

After I gave it to him, he told me to have a seat. I turned and sat in one of the fold-down wooden chairs in the front row. I noticed six, maybe seven police officers sitting in a jury box talking in low voices amongst themselves. Just the sight of their crispy blue uniforms made me sink a little lower in my seat. There was a long conference table up front with two attorneys on each end. I watched as the bailiff leaned over and whispered to a man who then turned around and looked at me.

He was young, around thirty, disheveled, with a wrinkled suit. He walked toward me, leaned over and said, "Let's go out in the hallway where we can talk." He seemed to be in hurry as I followed him out.

"How can I help you?"

"I'm Jerry Mendias' mother and I want to know what's going to happen to him?"

"Well, your son has agreed to a plea bargain of four years."

"Four years? But that's so long."

"Actually, it's not that bad considering...."

"It's not bad unless you're the one doing the four years."

He narrowed his beady blue eyes.

"I'd like to say something to the judge on my son's behalf?" I have no idea where this impulse came from. It was certainly not the plan, but I wanted to be there for him.

"It won't make a difference, if that's what you're thinking."

"It'll make a difference to me."

He studied me with one eye brow raised. He may have thought I was just some crazy mother going to throw herself on the mercy of the court for her son, but I wouldn't budge. I stared right back at him until he said, "Alright, I'll see what I can do."

We turned and went back inside. The courtroom was getting more crowded by the minute. I sat down and chewed on one of my finger nails wondering why I had just insisted on talking to the judge. What would I say? Would he recognize me?

All of the sudden the steel-belted-bailiff roared, "*Please rise for the Honorable Judge Aranda. Division B of Torrance Municipal court is now in session.*"

Everyone stood up as Judge Aranda entered through the back door dressed in sweeping black robes. He looked exactly like I remembered him, only he'd lost a bit of hair. When he sat down, he grabbed a file from a stack on the corner of his desk. He called the first case of the day and the court was in session.

As I listened to the proceedings of defendants, I started to notice a pattern with Judge Aranda. He was stipulating twelve-step meetings to the sentencing in most cases. Although he never did that with me, it still warmed my heart that he wanted to help people.

After a tedious morning of case after case, a Sheriff finally escorted Jerry into the room with his wrists cuffed behind his back. His brown eyes searched and when his gaze landed on me I smiled and waved the same way I did on his first day of school. He gave a weak smile as he was led to stand beside his public defender.

"Gerald Mendias, is that your true and legal name?" Judge Aranda's voice boomed.

"Yes, your Honor."

"You are being charged with assault with a deadly weapon. How do you plead?"

"Guilty, your honor."

I shifted uneasily in my chair. An eerie sensation rippled-up the back of my spine. It felt like I was peeking through a portal of time, back to when I stood in front of the judge. Only this time, it was like I was in the movie *Trading Places* and my son was taking my place in the leading role. A bitter taste of shame burned at the back of my throat. Clearly, history was repeating itself.

I was spiraling into harsh judgment of myself while the judge spewed out his legal jargon.

"It is the judgment of this court that the defendant, Gerald Mendias is guilty of the felony, assault with a deadly weapon and will serve four years in state prison."

It was all happening so fast. I could barely track what was going on. When the judge finished his long ramble of legal jargon, the public defender paused.

"The mother would like to address the court, Your Honor."

Aranda paused, then shrugged, "Sure, why not?"

My pulse took off like a gazelle. I took a deep breath and stood up.

Fuck. Fuck. Fuck. Shit. Shit. Shit.

I pushed past the swinging doors of the divider and stood up front. It felt like all my blood had halted inside my veins. I could feel the stares of everyone in that courtroom watching the crazy mother to see what she was going to do.

"So, you're the defendant's mother?" Aranda said.

"Yes, Your Honor."

"Go ahead."

"Well, you probably don't remember me Your Honor… but my name is Wendy Adamson. I appeared in front of you a long time ago. So first of all, I would like to make direct amends to you, and I also want to make amends to my son." I lifted one hand toward Jerry. "For what you see there is the direct result of my drug use."

Aranda leaned back with a smile on his face.

"Your Honor, although I circled the drain for many years, I'm finally sober now." My chest expanded as I took another deep breath. "But I've had a lot of help along the way. And those same people who have been there for me would be there for my son as well."

Jerry dropped his head. His shoulders shook as he openly sobbed. The whole court room was silent. You could hear the buzz of the air-conditioner.

Time seemed to slow down to a crawl. I was fully in my body. Present. Even though I was openly exposing myself and making myself vulnerable in front of cops, prosecutors and a judge, I didn't care. I thought I had to somehow tilt the cosmic forces toward ultimate justice by showing up for my son.

"Your Honor, if nothing can be done about the four-year sentence will the court please consider at the very least sending my son to a camp or minimum-security close by so I can go visit him?"

Judge Aranda leaned forward and said, "I want to congratulate you on your sobriety and commend you on the courage it took to stand in front this courtroom today."

"Thank you, Your Honor." My heart was pounding.

"While I may not be able to change your son's sentence, I will make a recommendation that he be sent somewhere close by."

He scribbled inside Jerry's chart. "Thank you so much, Your Honor"

"And Wendy, keep up the good work." He smiled.

"Yes, Your Honor. I will."

As Jerry was being led away, tears fell down his cheeks. My heart ached for him. I mouthed the words, "I love you." Before he was ushered out the back door he looked at me with such sad eyes and said, "I love you Mom." Then he was gone.

Once I was back in my car, the new sober version of Wendy totally lost her shit. It felt as if something had shifted and I was shot straight into the epicenter of grief. Pressing my forehead against the steering wheel, I sobbed. The tears felt like they were being pulled out of my sockets by the fistful. Without drugs, I felt everything. Everything I hadn't felt before.

The Sins of the Father

en's Central Jail looked like the medieval architecture straight out of the 12th century. A vault-like-complex with over 17,000 men crammed inside on any given day. Sprawling and complex as Los Angeles itself, it has been rated as one of the worst jails in the world.

As I approached the entrance there was already a line that led up a ramp. Girlfriends, mothers, fathers, aunts, uncles, children and babies in strollers, all coming to see their loved ones. I slipped into the back of the line and was overcome by the strong scent of perspiration that hung in the air. I discreetly held the cuff of my shirt over my mouth, doing my best not to breathe in any germs.

Once inside, I was asked to empty the contents of my pockets into a plastic, wicker basket. I had left my purse at home because I knew it would just be searched. A burly officer with a barrel of a body inspected my coins, keys and the pack of cigarettes that I dropped inside, while an officer with caramel skin waved me through a framed metal detector. Thankfully, the buzzer didn't go off and I was allowed to retrieve my belongings which I stuffed into the large pockets of my dark blue hoodie.

Making my way to a counter in the back, I tore off one of the visiting forms from a tablet. I used a golf-sized pencil to fill out Jerry's full name, his booking number, as well as my name and address. Then I got into another line.

When my turn finally came, I slid the form to a stern-looking Sheriff who sat on the other side of the chest-high counter. He grabbed it, barely looking at me. He punched in Jerry's booking number, one finger at a time, while staring at the screen of a clunky IBM computer. It had been a week since Jerry had gone to court. I held my breath hoping he hadn't been moved yet.

Inmates were often taken in the early morning hours to Wayside, Chino or other facilities in the state. I was relieved when he gave me a visitor's pass and told me to wait to be called.

Squeezing onto one of the wooden benches alongside an overweight Latina woman, I waited. A huge fan in the corner blasted hot, pungent air across the lobby. Some unrecognized names were called over the PA system. A mother across from me tried to comfort her baby who was wailing in distress. She tried stuffing a bottle of formula in the baby's mouth, but the baby just shook her head back and forth.

"Visitor for Jerry Mendias, report to number thirty-two in the visiting area," the PA system boomed.

I made my way to another check-point where I handed another sheriff my pass. He waved me in to the inner sanctum where a line of mushroom stools sprouted up in front of Plexiglas windows. Numbers were stenciled onto the floor in thick black paint. I walked down the aisle until I found Jerry, sitting on the other side of the glass. He gave me a weak smile as I sat down. He was starting to look healthy again. But it was so sad to see him in his county blues, knowing he was going to be locked-up for four years. My heart ached as I picked up the phone and held it to my ear.

"Hi Sweetie…" I pressed my hand against the thick glass.

"Hi Mom, how are you?"

"I'm okay, how are you?

"Guess who's in here?"

I figured it had to be one of his homeboys. "Who?" I said.

"Dad."

The blood seemed to stop dead in my veins.

"But, but I just saw him a couple weeks ago. "

"I know. He told me but he got arrested right after that."

"For what?"

"Some old warrant he had."

"Oh my God…."

He leaned in close to the window and whispered, "We're in the same cell together."

I shook my head. "No fucking way."

"I know. It's crazy, right? I can't even believe it myself."

"Did they put you two together because he's your father?"

"The cops don't have any idea we're related…."

"Oh my God…."

A small boy ran after a toy car he'd rolled on the floor behind me. His mother scolded him and told him to get back over to her. The caged fluorescent lights buzzed overhead.

"Sometimes when I watch Dad sleeping in the lower bunk it makes me cry."

Tears filled my eyes as I stared at Jerry through the Plexiglass window. Letting out a long sigh, I whispered into the phone. "I'm so sorry Jerry…."

A lump formed in the back of my throat. My whole body went hot. It felt like everything was breaking loose inside of me all at once. Then I had a crazy thought. What if Jerry and Max being there together wasn't a random coincidence at all? What if there was a divine intelligence who orchestrated an opportunity for a father and his son to heal by placing in them in the same cell? All of the sudden, what I had considered to be a tragedy, became an extraordinary event.

The Ripple Effect

When Rikki entered puberty, he went from being a kid who liked to snuggle to an obnoxious brat who didn't want me near his room. At the time he was attending Santa Monica High School which was three blocks away from where we lived. It was the first semester when I got a call asking me to come the principal's office.

As I sat down in a chair next to Rikki, Mr. Reed, the principal, was on the other side of his massive desk. It felt like there was an island between us. My foot tapped uncontrollably as I spun out worse case scenarios in my head. I may not have realized it back then, but I was getting a taste of what I put my dad through when I was a kid.

With a stern look on his face, Mr. Reed said, "We had an incident this morning with our school security guard who tried to stop some boys who were smoking marijuana. Rikki just so happened to with them."

My heart dropped. I looked over at Rikki.

He shook his head fiercely, "I wasn't smoking any Mom."

Mr. Reed interrupted. "We aren't saying you were Rikki, but we just want to know whats the names of the boys you were with?"

"I don't know who they are." He shrugged.

"You didn't know them, Rikki?" I asked.

"No, Mom. I was just walking alongside them and the security guard came rushing up to us. They ran, so I did too."

There was silence. I looked over at Mr. Reed because I certainly had no idea what to do or say. Mr. Reed picked up a paper on his desk and looked it over. "And why is it your grades are falling behind, Rikki?" I could hear annoyance in Mr. Reed's voice. "Is there something going on in the home?" He looked at me.

I shifted nervously in my seat. My face went hot. I tore on the loose skin of my cuticle. I felt the familiar loud hum of shame in my bones. I couldn't tell Mr. Reed that I had spent a year in jail for shooting my husband's mistress. That I was trying not to use drugs and it was fucking hard sometimes. Nor was I going to tell him that Rikki and I lived in a women and children's center because it was none of his god damn business. Instead, I simply said, "Rikki's father and I recently separated."

"Oh, I see."

I kept everything close to my chest and Rikki did the same. Little did I realize, I was laying the same groundwork that my dad had laid with me. Dad had told me not to talk about my mother and I expected Rikki not to talk to anyone about my tainted past.

As we walked home that day the cars rushed by. The sun burned bright yellow in the sky.

In between drags I turned and said, "If you're smoking weed, Rikki, I want you to stop."

"You should talk. You can't even stop smoking those nasty cigarettes."

His words hit me like a sledgehammer upside the head. I was a hypocrite. Rikki was holding up a mirror that was hard for me to look at. What made me think if I stopped doing drugs and alcohol that would be enough? As it turned out, the work had just begun.

Where There's Smoke

S itting at the kitchen table, I took a long drag off my cigarette, when I heard Rikki's footsteps come up behind me. I tried to blow the smoke out the window, but it came right back in my face.

"Mom, when are you going to quit?" He batted his hand in the air. "It's hard to breathe in here."

Rikki may have hated cigarettes, but what he didn't know was that I was beginning to hate them as well. I hated the house smelling like stale piss and the way people looked at me whenever I lit up in a public place.

"Get ready for school or you'll be late." I changed the subject.

Rikki stomped off to his room as I gazed out the window at the busy street below. It was another beautiful day in sunny Southern California and there were gorgeous people on bikes, roller blades and skateboards headed for the beach. I was pretty damn sure none of those people smoked. I knew that the oh-so-fabulous-Westsiders did yoga, juiced, and looked down their perfectly sculpted noses at someone like me. I stubbed out my cigarette and yanked the yellow-stained, curtain shut. I didn't need them to remind me of how unhealthy I might be.

After some deliberation, I decided I'd quit in a month. Until then, I would cram as many cigarettes into my waking hours as humanly possible.

When the day finally arrived, I proudly slam-dunked the empty pack of cigarettes into the trashcan. "This is it, Rikki. Your mom is going to quit smoking today."

"Well, it's about time." He was not impressed.

When Rikki went off to school, I tried to stay busy cleaning the apartment. I scrubbed the kick board and washed the linoleum floor on my knees with a scouring brush. I cleaned the refrigerator and defrosted the freezer. The place was sparkly and clean, but my anxiety had gotten worse. I paced the apartment with fingers clenched. A thin layer of sweat broke out on my skin. I wanted to scream out loud. By the time it was midday, I couldn't take it anymore. I headed for the store to buy a pack of cigarettes.

I confessed when Rikki got home from school. "I'm sorry, it was harder than I thought. I'll try again tomorrow."

He didn't say anything, but I could see the shadow of disappointment flash across his face. It made me feel like I was destined to remain a loser mom no matter what I did.

I tried over and over to quit, but it seemed impossible. I even started buying single cigarettes at the liquor store so I wouldn't have the temptation of an entire pack. I thought smoking in moderation was better, but I couldn't do anything moderately.

Then I remembered what Ruth once told me. *If you want to stop a bad habit, you have a better chance at success if you replace it with a healthy habit.'* That got me thinking, what if I tried exercise? At the time that was a radical and foreign concept for me.

I knew Rikki wore the same size shoe as me, so I had an idea. He was reclined on his bed, with his fingers flickering on the keys of his Nintendo controller. "Can I try on your roller blades?"

"What for?" He didn't even look at me.

"I just want to see if I can do it is all...."

"Oh Mom...you'll break your neck."

"I want to give it a try."

"There, in the closet."

"Rikki, I need your help getting them on."

Letting out a long, exasperated sigh, he paused his video game. "Alright, alright..." he said.

I grabbed his wrist guards and he grabbed his red roller blades before heading outside. I sat down on the bottom step and like Cinderella I extended my foot. Rikki loosened the strings on the boot, then slipped it on to my foot. "See, I told you, we are the exact same size."

Rikki shrugged while snapping the Velcro shut at the top. When both boots were on, I reached for his hand. "Okay, help me up."

When I stood up it felt like the wheels would slip right out from underneath me. My heart raced. I was slammed with panic. I thought I would fall and look like an idiot.

"You sure about this, Mom?"

"Yeah, yeah, I'm sure."

I rolled slowly along the sidewalk using Rikki's shoulder for support. As we turned the corner, there was a newly paved street which I knew would be perfect for my first trial run. I let go of Rikki and extended my arms like the bride of Frankenstein. I pushed-off one clunky blade at a time. Within seconds, I found a rhythm and was gliding along. It had to be all the ice-skating I used to do when I was kid, but there was no doubt, I was a natural born skater.

"Oh my God," I yelled. "Look! I'm doing it."

I glided to the corner, made a wide turn and headed back. I didn't know how to brake, so I rolled into Rikki's arms and thankfully, he was able to help me stop.

"I did it. I did it!"

"Pretty good Mom, for your first time."

That was all it took for me. The next day while Rikki was in school, I was stuffing a Walkman, cassettes and a pack of cigarettes into a fanny pack and strapping it around my waist before I headed out the front door to join the rest of the world.

As I made my way toward the beach, I kept a keen eye out for cracks in the cement. By the time I got down to the bike path, I was so winded I felt like I had run a marathon.

As I sat on a bench for a moment to take it all in, I was mesmerized by the brilliant blue sky and the vast ocean that sparkled like cut glass. Seagulls drifted overhead, while a few surfers took their chances by cutting into a small wave. It was breathtaking. I had a realization. This was the reason why all those Westsides went by my window every day. They wanted to be a part of all of this.

After a few minutes, I rolled back onto the bike path. Deciding to test my limits, I picked up as much speed as I possibly could. Pushing off on my blades, the muscles in my legs tightened while my arms swung back and forth like pendulums. I was going pretty fast when a cute guy with dark hair and tattoos came up alongside me. He was a fine specimen of male athletic ability. As he zoomed by, he flashed me an unexpected smile before disappearing into a speck of dust down the path. I can't emphasize enough what that smile did for my low self-esteem. Ever since Max had left me, I felt invisible, but that rolling smile meant I had been seen.

Deciding to take a break, I plopped down on a patch of grass and reached inside my fanny pack for a cigarette. But as I inhaled, I felt once again like a hypocrite. There I was trying to get fit by exercising while puffing away on a cancer stick. It seemed one canceled out the other.

After that, I tried countless more times to stop but I still couldn't do it. Eventually I turned to prayer. 'God please remove this obsession to self-destruct with cigarettes.' I was about to give up, until one morning I heard a voice speaking with absolute authority inside my head, '*QUIT NOW!*' it said. So, I tried again. Only this time, it was different than before- it felt like I had some unseen help. Don't get me wrong. I still had cravings, but they weren't nearly as bad as they had been in the past. Ultimately, I was willing to quit because I wanted to be a better mom.

Long Lost Sister

I hadn't spoken to my sister in ten years so, you can imagine my surprise when I picked up the phone, "Hi, it's Diane… your sister." It seemed like she thought I might have forgotten who she was.

My breath caught in my throat. "Oh, hey Diane. How are you?"

The last time I saw my sister was in the mid-eighties when I got off the plane in San Francisco. I started drinking before the flight and was fucked-up by the time I got there. Honestly, I can't even tell you what happened that night, but when I woke up the next morning with a pounding headache, Diane was standing by the bed with her hands on her hips.

"I'm sending you back to LA." Her lips were pulled tight.

"Why? What's wrong?"

"You were a complete idiot last night. You embarrassed me in front of Kenny."

Diane met Kenny in the Peace Corps and married soon after they were done. My visit was for us to finally get to meet. By Diane's reaction, it seemed as if I might not have made a good impression.

"I think you're an alcoholic, Wendy. You need to get some help."

I was outraged. How dare she call me an alcoholic! My dad was an alcoholic. But not me. Besides, who was she to talk? She used to drink like a fish.

We drove to the airport in silence and I hadn't seen or heard from her since.

"Someone told me you're sober now?" Diane voice sounded laced with doubt.

"Yup. Stone-cold-sober. That's me."

"That's really cool."

"Who would have thought? Right?"

Our first conversation was awkward. I didn't know what to say, so I started asking about her life. Diane told me she was an RN now, taking care of mentally ill people in a San Francisco hospital. On her days off, to counteract her taxing job in a psych unit, she'd use her high energy and obsessive nature to compete in triathlons. I was impressed that she seemed to have moved on from our dysfunctional upbringing and had what appeared to be a rich and meaningful life.

After that, Diane started calling me every week. Having a relationship with my sister as an adult was totally foreign for me. As kids we were always trying to just survive.

Diane gave me an update on my two brothers. Jay, the eldest, who was the schizophrenic, was MIA but possibly living in Hollywood. No one knew for sure. Our youngest brother, Bruce was supposedly homeless and living in his truck somewhere in northern California. My heart hurt for all my siblings. It was clear that there was a lot of damage done that caused us to splinter off in different directions because we were never given any tools.

I ended up telling my sister about the boy who got shot in front of my apartment. And even though it still felt strange to talk about it, I told Diane about the light that came to me later when I was trying to go to sleep.

"Oh my God. It sounds like you had a spiritual experience of some sort," she exclaimed.

"All I know is that experience changed me somehow."

"I bet it did."

"It's like once I knew there was more-I couldn't go back to not knowing."

"You know what. I've recently started meditating and it helps me to stay in the moment," Diane said.

"I don't think I could sit still long enough to meditate."

"You'd be surprised how easy it is when you have support."

Diane told me she was going to a place called the Siddha Center where people meditated and chanted in Sanskrit together. It all seemed way too bizarre for me. As an addict, meditation had never been on my radar. Who can sit still for one minute if you're amped-up on meth?

Diane continued. "I want to gift you a meditation intensive for an entire weekend."

"That sounds like a really long time to sit still Diane."

"They take plenty of breaks in between and there's a cafeteria and you can go home each night."

"I don't know Diane…"

"I checked and they are having one right by your house in a couple weeks."

Being a people pleaser at heart, I didn't want to disappoint my sister. Especially since she'd just come back into my life.

"I'll give it a go." I said, giving in.

The intensive started early Saturday morning. Rikki was old enough to be on his own now, so I told him I'd be back in time dinner.

The Siddha Center was less than a mile away. I walked over there when the sun was coming up. It was a squatty building and didn't look spiritual or churchy at all. Honestly, I was having second thoughts, but I forged on because my sister had paid for it in advance.

There were a few hostesses sitting at a table. "I'm here for the intensive," I said.

"Welcome." She bowed her head.

I returned a small smile.

"Are you new to Siddha?"

"It's my first time."

"Welcome to our Center. If you like, we have a light breakfast going on in the Cafeteria, if you want to get a bite to eat."

I pinned the badge with my name on it to my sweater, then walked to the cafeteria where I found groups of bead-wearing hippies in flowing attire who were drinking tea. Some of them had lamb skin rugs or Himalayan blankets by their sides and I shamelessly judged them all.

When a delicate bell chimed, everyone got up at the same time to make their way to the meditation room. Not knowing what was going on, I just followed along. After I took off my shoes I was greeted by a woman with long braids in her hair. She bowed her head before leading me to sit on a pillow in the front of the massive hall.

Diane had already explained to me that it is a Hindu tradition to divide men and women on opposite sides of the room. This way we'd focus on connecting with a higher power, rather than finding a date.

As I waited for the ceremonies to get started, I shivered with the streams of cold air blasting through the vents above. The guru was late. God dammit! I shifted the cheeks of my ass on the pillow as I grew impatient. After all, if you're a guru, at the very least you can be on time.

All of a sudden, a hushed silence fell across the room and everyone stood up. I watched, intrigued as a stunning Indian woman with coal-black hair and sparkling almond eyes glided past in a blast of orange robes. I had always thought gurus had skinny arms and round beach ball bellies. Another misconception I had. Gurumayi was beautiful. Not what I had expected at all.

She stepped onto a platform in the front and adjusted her robes all around as she lowered herself onto a maroon velvet chair. When she was settled, a pretty teenager dressed in a traditional Indian garb, came in the back of the room holding a tray of small candles. Everyone burst into a song. The Arati that they knew by heart. A group of musicians sat on the floor playing music. It all seemed very cultish to me. It's a wonder I didn't run.

Then the Guru, in perfect English started talking. "With deep love and respect, I welcome you with all my heart and soul." She lowered her head and everyone did the same.

What surprised me the most was how well the Guru articulated her message. Gurumaya said, that in the absence of forgiveness, that whatever happened to us in our past will keep replaying in our minds, causing more anger. This can often result in bitterness and bad health. She also said, if we don't forgive those people we are resentful at, we can't move on with our lives.

When she was done, she told us we were going to chant. Everyone sang back and forth, using call and response with the mantra, *Om Namah Shivaya*. I was doing my best to keep an open mind, but chanting felt like a bit of a stretch for a dope fiend like myself. My head started once again to swirl in judgment until I remembered a quote I had recently heard: "There is a principal against all information, keeping a man in everlasting ignorance— that principal is contempt prior to investigation."

Then it occurred me, I not only had contempt for the intensive, but I had preconceived notions for just about everything in life. At that instant, I willed myself to suspend all judgment and see what happened. In other words, I chose to give the intensive a chance.

Within minutes, I found myself chanting along with everyone else. *Om Namah Shivaya. Om Namah Shivaya,* coming from deep within my diaphragm. I got so into it, it felt like I was being carried in a cloud of sound with everyone else. What I would later learn is that chanting quiets down the chatter in your head.

After thirty minutes, it was time to meditate. I adjusted my butt, trying to get comfortable on the thin pillow. Somehow, I slipped into a quiet place. I'm not quite sure how much time had passed, but all of a sudden images burst into my brain like uninvited guests. Scenes from my childhood swooped in on me like strangers in some dark alley. Flashbacks crashed into one another behind the curtains of my eyelids.

At first they were coming so fast I could barely make sense of it all. But eventually it all slowed down and I saw myself as a small, frightened little girl. My mother, eyes wild, coming toward me with a bar of Ivory soap clutched in her hand. We were in a small bathroom where she stuffed the soap in my mouth. A tightness clenched my throat and I gagged, which made her shove it in even deeper. My knees jangled like two loose spoons as I clutched my fists, nails digging into my palms. "You are a bad girl. A very, very bad girl," my mother snarled. I think that may have been when my spirit broke because I believed my mother. I was a bad girl because I had terrible thoughts like wishing she were dead. I was a bad girl and from then on I would let this inner badness direct my life.

Just as quickly as those images appeared, they receded like landmarks in a rear-view mirror. My breath was deep. The energy intense. What the hell just happened, I wondered? Nothing made sense. I crossed and re-crossed my legs, trying to get comfortable. I could hear the soft hum of the harmonium. The soothing sound made the room feel like it was breathing. I looked around. Everyone had their eyes closed. Didn't they understand what had just happened to me? They looked peaceful while I was having my own horror flick going on inside my brain. *Okay, calm down*, I told myself. I forced myself to close my eyes again. Eventually it felt like time slowed down as I was able to get beyond my brain, beyond the voice inside my head.

It somehow never occurred to me what my mother must have felt like when she started having mental breakdowns. With my eyes still closed I somehow slipped into her skin, I felt how scared she must have been, I lowered my face into my hands. I don't know if anyone heard me cry, but I allowed myself to grieve for her. And as I laid claim to the part of me that I had repressed, I didn't run. I let the feelings come. Then, at some point, I felt a bottomless sense of peace. Stillness. And I didn't run.

Comparing Notes

Diane couldn't wait to hear my thoughts on the intensive, calling me Sunday when it was over.

"It was amazing..." I said.

"You liked it?" Her voice had a hint of surprise.

"All except the flash backs I had."

"From childhood?"

I took a long sigh. "Do you ever think about what happened back then?"

"I try not to, but yes, I have..."

"How the hell did we ever survive it all?"

Up until then we'd both avoided talking about our childhood. I used drugs to forget. Diane used excessive exercise. But now it was time to start talking about the things no one spoke of in our house.

"Do you remember when I cut my wrist?" I said.

"Who could forget that?" Diane replied.

I was fifteen and had stayed out all night. When I came home, Dad called me a whore. The word made me coil up inside, turned my brain good, and red. I didn't say a word. Instead, I went into the bathroom, picked up a double-edge razor blade and swiped the razor blade across my wrist like a credit card. The debt had become due. I cut at my dad. I cut to punish him. I cut to make him pay. I cut because we had somehow entered into a twisted power struggle. A warped chess game, pitting daughter against father, where no one would ever win. I remember a fleeting moment of satisfaction as I watched the flesh open in a scream. Two exposed rope-like tendons with blood flowing like a red ribbon. Satisfaction was instantly replaced by concern as I walked out with my arm extended, careful not get blood on my 501 jeans. I was rushed to the emergency room where I was stitched up, and later I was admitted to Camarillo State Mental Hospital, the same place mother had been many times before.

I let out a long sigh as I recalled the event with my sister.

"You seemed to be following in mom's footsteps," Diane said.

"That's what Dad used to tell me all the time."

As we talked about these things, Diane and I were like survivors of a shipwreck sifting through the wreckage of our childhoods. We were two broken women talking about things no one ever acknowledged when we were growing up. Diane escaped with excessive exercise, I escaped with drugs. Yet here it was. We were standing next to each other on dry land. What were the chances of that?

The Family System

By the time Rikki was in his teens he was falling behind in school. With Jerry in prison I was afraid I might be losing another son. In an attempt to keep my eye on Rikki, I started making him attend a Friday night meeting with me.

"Mom I don't want to go."

"You have to go."

"But they're so boring."

"We can go to the Promenade after and hang out." My first go-to was to bribe him.

"Can I get some shoes then?"

"Why does everything have to be about shoes?"

The packed meeting was held in a church auditorium. When we arrived, Rikki and I weaved through the clusters of smoking hipsters out front and headed downstairs. There was a fresh-faced enthusiastic greeter at the door. I smiled and said hello as Rikki trailed behind me with arms crossed in front of his chest. After we found a couple of seats in the back row, we settled in. I scanned the room for cute guys. While I had a couple quick flings early in sobriety, I always felt like I couldn't sustain a relationship because of Rikki. I didn't want to be one of those moms who paraded a series of men through the home. But on the other hand, I could have an entire romantic interlude inside my brain without anyone knowing.

"Do we have to stay for the whole meeting?" Rikki asked.

"We just got here."

"I'm already bored."

The first speaker that night was a thirty-something guy with tattoos and spikey black hair. The audience was cracking-up as he laid out his personal debacle of blackouts, arrests, and random sex with strangers. To normal people, killing yourself on the installment plan isn't necessarily funny, but if you're an alcoholic you laugh because you usually relate. The speaker was hysterical and had everyone laughing. Rikki? Not so much. Every time a punch line landed he would go, "HA, HA, HA." The people in front of us turned their heads to see who the obnoxious kid was behind them. Shame prickled at the base of my neck. Mortified, I whispered through tight lips, "Rikki stop it."

"Can we go home then?"

"NO. Not till the meeting is over."

Clearly, he was punishing me. When the audience roared again with laughter Rikki did the same thing. "Ha, Ha, Ha." I lowered myself in my seat.

When it was time for the break, I was relieved. I would give Rikki a good what-for outside. But as he followed me out the door, we were stopped dead in our tracks as a sleek black and gray dog reared-up on Rikki's chest with a very cute guy holding the end of the leash. He was medium height, in loose jeans, a t-shirt and a golden hoodie tied around his waist. His face was tan and he had freckles sprinkled across the bridge of his nose.

"I think my dog likes you." His smile revealed perfect teeth.

"What's his name?" Rikki asked.

"That's Goldie and I'm Ronnie."

I squatted and stroked Goldie's thick soft fur. In return I got licked on my cheek.

"Beautiful dog."

"That's what I'm told."

"So how long you been around Ronnie?" I asked.

"I've been sober twenty years."

"Wow. You must have been really young."

"Yeah, I suppose. But I was a troubled teenager when a big-brother-type found me and took me under his wing."

Rikki was petting Goldie when Ronnie extended the leash. "You want to hold him?"

"Really?"

"Yep."

"My son may not like meetings, but he certainly loves dogs," I said.

"The meetings are boring," Rikki chimed in.

Ronnie nodded. "I know what you mean, buddy. That's why I hang out here. I come mostly to see my friends after it's over."

Rikki looked at me. "Can I stay out here with Ronnie, Mom?"

"I don't know if…"

Ronnie lifted his hands. "It's fine by me. We'll stay right here where you can keep an eye on us."

"Okay. Sure. Why not?" I shrugged.

I was able to hear the second speaker and watch them through the glass doors so it worked out well. After the meeting, we said our good byes and I figured I probably wouldn't see Ronnie again. But he was there every Friday, and soon Rikki started looking forward to seeing him and his dog each week. At one point Ronnie asked if he could join us for a walk when the meeting was over. "Sure," I said.

We strolled over to the Promenade where the movie-goers, street acts, shoppers and runaway kids would hang out in droves. All of a sudden, Rikki saw a pair of sneakers on display and ran over to get a closer look.

"Look at these fresh Nikes." He pointed at a pair of Michael Jordan's in the display window.

"I'm sure they cost a fortune."

"Those are really cool alright," Ronnie said.

Rikki had become obsessed with name brand shoes, which I couldn't afford. Although I was still filing medical charts, my paychecks at the doctor's office were barely enough to make ends meet.

"Let's keep it moving, guys."

As we walked, Ronnie asked, "I wanted to see if I could come over and play video games with Rikki this weekend?"

"Please, Mom?"

Rikki had absolutely no male role-models in his life and I figured he could really use one. While I was normally suspicious,

I knew Ronnie had a solid reputation because I had asked people within my growing recovery community.

"Yeah. Sure," I said.

That Sunday, Ronnie came over the first time. I was embarrassed because the place was sparsely decorated. I hadn't hung anything on the walls because that felt like a commitment and I still wasn't sure I was going to be sticking around.

"I haven't had time to fix it up yet..."

Ronnie waved a dismissive hand. "Oh, please. You should see my bachelor pad."

Rikki and Ronnie played Nintendo in the living room. Within minutes they had sat on the floor, laughing with their fingers darting all over their control pads.

I had no idea at the time that Ronnie would play such a key figure in Rikki's life. No idea that over the following years, he would take Rikki roller blading, to the movies, and even buy him those Michael Jordan sneakers we saw in the window. Ronnie's stability, guidance and love helped me get through Rikki's tumultuous teens. Whenever Rikki did get in trouble, I'd ask Ronnie to have a talk with him. It was hard to explain to friends who thought Ronnie was cute, why I didn't jump his bones. Not that Ronnie would have slept with me anyway, but in my mind their relationship was sacred. I didn't want to be the mother who sabotaged it. Not only was the friendship important to Rikki, but later Ronnie would also give Jerry a job when he was released from prison. How do you thank someone who impacts both your sons like that? Certainly not by sleeping with him.

Brother's Keeper

Diane called me and the first thing out of her mouth was, "Are you sitting down?" My heart took off like a gazelle.

"Why? What's wrong?"

"Jay is dead," she blurted out.

"Oh my god...how?" I hadn't seen my schizophrenic brother for over a decade and had no idea where he lived or what he was doing.

"Not really sure, but the coroner's office called Bruce and said he was dead for two weeks inside his apartment before anyone found him."

"Holy shit!" It felt like the breath was stuck in my throat.

"You have to go empty out his apartment," Diane said.

"But, wha, what, do I do?"

"Just go through his things, pack them up, throw them away, I don't care."

"I've never done anything like that before."

"Compared to everything else you've been through I'm sure you can manage."

Okay. So, I wanted to show Diane how I could do anything now that i was sober, but Jay had always scared me. Growing up he was, not only creepy, he was often mean to me. As the oldest of the two boys, he was a bully and when he got mad he scared everyone in the house. One time during an argument with my Dad, he pulled a machete out on him. Another time he tried to burn the house down by making a bonfire with his briefs in the middle of his bedroom.

It wasn't until he was diagnosed as a paranoid-schizophrenic that things started to make sense. It was the late sixties and a lot of people were tripping on acid but Jay took it even a step further. As a chemistry major at Santa Monica City college, Jay decided to create his own make-shift lab in his closet and manufactured LSD himself. To keep Dad from snooping around, he put a huge padlock on the bedroom door. Apparently, Jay knew the chemical compounds of LSD and of course, he had to try the product himself to see if it was any good. Soon, things got really weird. One night, I was watching television when everyone else was sleeping. Jay came in, his crossed eyes opened wide. "Wendy, come look, Martians just landed outside my window."

An icy chill ran up my spine. My heart raced. Should I scream for help? Should I run? Instead, I just said, "Ah, that's okay. I'm watching something right now, Jay." I nodded at the television set.

I used to wonder what might have happened if Dad had sought the help of a therapist or psychiatrist? But nothing was ever addressed in our house. Instead Diane and I grew more and more afraid of our older brother who seemed psychotic. We started propping up a chair against the doorknob of our bedroom so he wouldn't chop us to bits while we were asleep.

It all came to a head when the cops kicked in the front door and went straight for Jay's bedroom lab. We all watched from the hallway sleepy-eyed as Jay was handcuffed and hauled-off to jail under arrest for manufacturing lysergic acid diethylamide. For hours the cops meticulously dismantled his lab, labeling each chemical and glass vial for evidence in court.

Detective Eubanks asked my Dad how come he didn't intervene on Jay beforehand.

"We could smell the chemicals out in the hallway," he said.

"I didn't smell a thing." Dad had built a wall of denial to protect himself from any truth.

Jay would end up serving three years in Atascadero State Hospital for the criminally insane. After that, he was on disability for the rest of his life.

Since Jay was dead for over two weeks in his apartment, I was afraid to go alone. So, I called my friend Emma, and asked her to go with me for support. The following Saturday morning Emma and I parked in front of Jay's housing complex. My stomach was doing flip-flops. We watched a disheveled man come out of the building clutching the front of his heavy coat together. A flasher, no doubt.

"Let's get it over with." I pushed opened the car door.

We walked side by side up the pathway. When we got the gate, I pushed the button and a buzzer sounded. There was a hollow click and the lock released. I leaned in with my shoulder to open the gate. Inside the lobby I was hit with the smell of mold and piss. An icy chill crawled up my spine and spread across my shoulder blades. I stopped at the office and approached a woman with coffee skin sitting in a small cubicle that was her office.

"Can I help you?"

"I'm Jay Adamson's sister. I'm here to go through his things."

"Oh. Hello. I'm very sorry for your loss." She seemed sincere.

"Thank you... Are you the one who found him?"

"No. Unfortunately, I was on vacation at the time or else I would have noticed he hadn't been around. It pains me to think he was in there for two whole weeks before they discovered him."

"I haven't had contact with Jay for a long time. How was he doing before? I mean was he still, ah, you know... suffering?"

"Jay was fine as long as he took his meds. But when he didn't take his meds he'd start hearing the voices."

"The voices?"

"Yup. I keep an eye on everyone who lives here. When I wouldn't see Jay around for a while I would go to his door and sometimes, I could hear him talking to demons."

"Demons?"

"Yup. He called them demons all right. I'd have to warn him, he was at risk of losing his apartment if he didn't start taking his meds."

Jay was just like my mother. Whenever she took her meds she could function, but if she stopped, she'd suffer a psychotic break.

I paused, shifting back and forth on my feet.

"His apartment number is 211. Here's the key. You can bring it back when you're done. The elevator is to your left." She pointed.

"Okay, thanks so much for your help." We walked over and pushed the button.

Emma held my arm. "Are you okay?"

"I don't know. I'm not sure."

We stepped inside the elevator and when the door shut, all of the sudden I felt trapped. My heart was racing. My skin felt prickly. I felt a gripping inside my chest. I wanted to run back to my car. The fear was the same type I felt living with Jay and my mother when I was a child. But why? Jay was dead. He couldn't chop me into tiny bits. Then why was it my knees trembled and I was breaking out into a sweat?

"Look." I held out a my shaking hand to show Emma.

"I'm here with you. It's going to be okay."

"But this, this isn't normal. My brother's dead."

My chest hammered with panic. I had suppressed these feelings with drugs for so long, that sober, they often felt foreign to me. I knew my feelings were irrational but I couldn't reason my way out of it. I was overwhelmed and wanted to run but, when the elevator doors opened, my feet took me down the corridor until I was standing in front of his apartment. I stared blankly at the door, then slipped in the key. I took a deep breath. As soon as I stepped inside I caught the edge of Jay's scent along with a rancid odor of rotting meat with a hint of cheap cologne. It was the smell of death. But this wasn't just a random death. It was my brother's death. Memories of Jay came flooding into my present. I wanted to run. Emma said something but, it felt like I was in a wind tunnel and couldn't make it out. An invisible magnet was pulling me straight toward the bedroom. Against the wall was a full-size mattress with box spring with no sheets or blankets on it. In the center of it was large brownish-black stain. My stomach churned. I wanted to throw up. Chills ran up my spine.

"Oh my God. That's where he died," I whispered. "He was alone."

Jay had perished on that mattress cut off from family and probably didn't have any friends. How frigging sad was that? He was only living a few miles away from me and I didn't even know it. Our parallel lives had clicked along like two trains beside each other with similar routes but different destinations.

"Maybe we should start in the other room?" Emma said, placing a gentle hand on my shoulder. I nodded and we went back to the living room. I stood a moment and looked at the single worn, black chair that faced the television. That was where he must have been where he spent his time. Watching television just like dad used to do.

When I touched a small clock on a dresser it was covered with a thin layer of grease. I remembered Jay loved hamburgers. I imagined that's all he probably ate. Maybe his arteries were blocked with so much plaque his heart just gave out? I wondered if his life flashed in front of his eyes and what would that have looked like if it did? Did he think about mom and dad? Did he think about his childhood? Did he think of me?

I walked to the kitchen where the linoleum stuck beneath my shoes. I opened a creaky brown cabinet and instead of finding food, there were rows of old VHS tapes, like Die Hard, The Good, The Bad and The Ugly and other films. Was this the way Jay lived? Psych meds, greasy burgers, and violent films? Time slowed to a crawl. I felt ashamed. I was embarrassed. Disgusted by how my brother had lived. I didn't want to touch anything. It was gross. My knees jangled together. The walls felt like they were closing in on me.

"I've got to get out of here." I turned toward the front door. Emma followed me. "Are you okay?"

"I can't do this. I can't go through this shit."

"You don't have to…"

"They can throw it all away as far as I'm concerned. It's too damn much…"

For days after that, while everything looked the same in my life, I felt a heaviness weighing on my chest. It was a deep and unexplainable sadness. Not only for Jay, but for my entire family. The feeling went on and on for weeks. There was a darkness that lingered around me like a cloud.

One night while sleeping, I saw Jay in my dream. He was standing in the corner of my room watching me. When I looked over at him, he simply said, "Hello Wendy." It caused me to shoot straight up in bed sweating with a thin layer of sweat. It totally freaked me out.

If new sobriety wasn't hard enough now, it felt like my ancestors were haunting me. Was the veil to the other side so thin that family members stuck around? If I were to be honest, hadn't I been haunted by my mother all my life? If I wanted to stay sober I would need somebody to help me navigate through the bleak darkness I was in.

Healing Trauma

When I called my friend Shari who I had met at the meditation center I was desperate. Shari was a healer who lived in the nearby mountains. She had exotic features, a voluptuous figure and looked like she could have walked off the pages of a *Vogue* magazine. I often wondered how someone so beautiful could heal people? But I knew countless individuals who had gone to her and swore that Shari had a gift.

"I've been in a really dark place since my brother died," I told her on the phone. "I don't understand it because we weren't even close."

"That doesn't matter. Everyone has ties with their family members that go back for generations. Your ancestors exist in many different realities. They even exist inside your blood, your genes. and in the spiritual world around you."

Although everything she said sounded strange, I made an appointment to see her. After I hung up the phone I immediately started second-guessing myself. How would an energy healer help me? Wasn't it just more woo-woo crap? Didn't I need a psychiatrist who could give me antidepressants to numb the constant ache I had in my chest. For some reason I didn't go that route. And in spite of my skepticism, a few days later I found myself driving up the windy road that looped through the canyons.

When I pulled up, Shari, who was waiting for me, had on tight-fitting designer jeans and a floral-hippie shawl. Her brown hair was threaded with golden streaks that cascaded over her shoulders. When I got out of the car she gave me a long embrace.

"I wasn't sure you'd make it." Shari raised a perfectly arched eyebrow.

"I almost didn't."

I followed her into the yellow cottage with white trim. As I entered, the first thing I saw was a majestic view of rust-colored mountains out the window. Flute music was playing and drifted around us like a cloud of sound. As I sat down, Shari handed me herbal tea. The cup felt warm as I took a sip.

"So, what's going on with you Wendy?"

"I wish I knew. I'm a total mess."

The words felt stuck in my throat. I had been a badass for so long it was still not normal for me to be vulnerable with anybody. But since my brother's death, another layer of my inner façade had started to crack.

"Do you think it's some early trauma you experienced when you were young?"

"No," I said, defensively. "Well maybe…? I really don't know anymore."

"Sometimes things get stored inside our bodies, and we don't even realize it's there."

"All I know is the feelings I had at Jay's apartment seemed ancient and old."

"I understand," Shari said, standing up with a look of concern on her face. "We should get started. We have some work to do."

She took me to a back room where gauze curtains blew like white flags of surrender on an afternoon breeze. I crawled up and lay down on the massage table that was already set up. When I closed my eyes, Shari covered me with a fuzzy blanket. What she didn't know I was battling a self-defeating mind that told me I had made a huge mistake. Thankfully, another voice kicked in telling me to: *Stay open. Stay open. Stay open.* As Shari took both my feet in her hands and took a deep breath, in spite of the mind chatter, my body started to relax. I started to hear the trickle of water from a small fountain outside. Chimes tinkled softly in the breeze. I was starting to drift when Shari placed her hot hand on top of my chest.

"Your heart feels as if it's encased in a shell."

My poor little broken heart. The heart that I had been trying to protect all my life. I was tired of being guarded. I was tired of being encased in my own shell.

When Shari placed her other hand on my sternum, my whole body started to tremble under the touch. I tried to will myself to stop shaking, but I couldn't.

"What the hell is going on with me?"

"It's stored up fear in your body being released."

"Oh shit…"

My mind traveled back to when my mother would have her psychotic breaks. I was so terrified of her I would curl up inside my bed and hide beneath my sheets. I remember feeling so small, so alone, and so afraid. On Shari's table it was the same feelings I used to experience back then as a child. Although I had started talking about my childhood with a sponsor and a few friends, I always felt so cut off from any emotions regarding it. But trauma can't always be reached by talking about it, because it's embodied in your cells.

My stomach felt clenched-up in a tight fist. A blackness like hot oily lava erupted inside my heart and spread across my chest. Tears started to fall down the edges of my face. All of the sudden I heard a painful moan escape from my lips. It was so primal. So old, I wasn't even sure if it came from me. And seconds later Shari was moaning right along with me. We sounded like two wounded animals caught inside a trap. Her matching the tone of my anguish was symbiotic in nature, but something I still find hard to explain with mere words. It was almost like she was there to escort me through dark corridors of years of stored up trauma. Then just as quickly we both fell into silence. Until moments later, Shari said, "Your mother is here."

My eyes fluttered open. "What did you say?"

"She's here. She wants you to know she loves you…."

My heart no longer felt encased in a shell as tears streamed down my face.

"Your mother was suffering in this realm and that's why she left you."

"You can talk to her?"

"It's more like she's downloading information to me."

"Will you, um, tell her… that I love her too…"

Shari smiled. "I think she already knows."

It was two hours when Shari finished working on me. When I found myself sitting at her dining room table I felt altered. Different somehow.

"That was incredible," I said, shaking my head.

"You should start feeling better now."

"Sometimes I think I'll never completely heal from the past."

"You're healing right now."

"But will it ever be done?"

"Unfortunately, we always have more work to do," She smiled, dimples cutting into her cheeks.

I was forty-one and I had just starting to grieve my mother's death. I had once thought if I got sober the universe would absolve me from any more pain. But when I stopped using drugs, all that repressed grief bubbled up to the surface. It was truly a miracle I didn't medicate. As much as I may have wanted to check out, I stayed present for it all.

Crossing Paths

O ne evening after work I was walking along the board-walk in Santa Monica when I spotted Max sitting with a girl (not the one I shot) on a bench. I had no idea he was even out of jail.

The girl was laughing with her blond hair falling like two curtains around her face. Max was animated, his hands dancing in the air as he talked. I was about to turn around when he saw me and jumped up. "Wendy!" He rushed over and gave me a big hug. He had put on some weight and looked much healthier than the last time I saw him.

"When did you get out?" I asked.

"A month ago… I was going to call you, but I've been trying to get on my feet first."

He turned to face the new blond. "This is Lisa." He paused. Looked back to me. "This is my ex-wife, Wendy."

Lisa stood up and extended her hand. "Oh, I've heard all about you."

Oh. I bet you did, I thought.

Narrowing my eyes, I glared at Max.

"It was all good stuff," Lisa said. "But I really feel like I know you now."

I smiled weakly.

"I'm clean now." Max changed the subject.

"Really?"

"Yup. I got eighteen months." Max puffed out his chest.

"That's awesome Max."

"I thought if you could do it maybe I could as well."

I chuckled. "I guess you're right. It is nothing short of a miracle." I paused. Then asked, "Hey, whatever happened to Cat?"

"She hooked-up with someone else while I was in jail and from what I hear she is living in Lomita and still getting high."

I thought back on the dirty, twitchy, tweaking, lifestyle of being a meth head. Staying up all night, running with losers. A chill ran up my spine just thinking about it. "Do you have her phone number?"

"Why do you want her number?"

"I want to make amends for shooting her."

"Do you think she'll even talk to you?" He looked at me sideways.

"I guess I'll find out."

He reached into his back pocket. "I can give you the old number I have. I don't know if it still works." Max pulled out a small spiral note pad and flipped through it as Lisa watched. I'm sure she was intrigued that we were being so civil to one another after all that had happened.

"Have you heard from Jerry at all?" he asked.

"He calls me every week and we've been writing each other."

"He's so far away and I don't have a car or I'd go see him."

"I sent him a package with a bunch of stuff that he wanted."

"There's nothing like getting a care package from your mom while in prison."

"Well, I got to get going," I said.

"I'll come by and see Rikki's this week."

"Cool." I tucked Cat's number in my front pocket. "See you around."

Things are always changing whether one realizes it or not. There's the natural erosion of the shores and the mountains, earthquakes and the unending geological process as Earth's po-larity flip back and forth. But in that moment, I couldn't help but notice how much I had changed. It had been three years since I'd gotten out of jail. I was off welfare, off probation had friends but even more astounding, seeing Max with another woman hadn't even affected me. It was clear to me I was moving on with my life.

Identity Crisis

S tanding in front of our shared closet, I couldn't find any-thing to wear to a sober party I was invited to. I owned hoodies, sweatshirts and baggy pants, but my clothes all seemed to blend in with Rikki's teenage apparel. Not a dress or a dainty blouse in sight. As I grabbed my favorite flannel hoodie, I stood in front of the mirror and tried to take an objective look at myself for the first time. I was starting to notice other wom-en my age didn't dress like I did. Who the hell was I anyway? It turned out I had absolutely no fucking clue.

I needed to do a complete overhaul, but that would take money and know-how, and I had neither. If only I could get on one of those television makeovers shows where a stylist could come-up with a new and improved version of me. It may have taken a lot of courage to get sober, but what would it take to dress age-appropriate. Time would tell. But meanwhile, I needed some clear-cut direction, so I called Camille, a girlfriend with a great sense of style.

"I don't know who I am anymore or how I'm supposed to dress." I let out a long-exasperated sigh.

"Oh. That. Well, yeah. We all go through that when we get sober but I can help you."

"Really? But how?"

"Come over and we can find something that works."

"Thank you, girl."

First thing Saturday morning I knocked on Camille's door. Camille had an athletic body and jet-black hair. When she let me in, I was stunned by the size of her living room with its white sofa, sleek coffee table and an abstract orange and green painting hanging against the back wall. Shafts of light came in from win-dows, cutting squares onto the polished hardwood floors. It was so luxurious compared to my small, dingy apartment with all its second hand, worn out furniture.

"I pulled a few things out for you to try on." Camille gestured for me to follow her.

As I walked down the hallway I let my hand brush over a mahogany wood beam. Maybe some of her good taste would rub off on me. Camille's bedroom had a four-poster king size bed and already laid on top was a pantsuit, a slinky black dress, a floral crepe blouse and other items.

"Why don't you try this on?" Camille handed me an elegant green and brown chiffon blouse. "You can use the bathroom for privacy if you want."

"That's okay. I'm used to dressing in front of other women. I had to do it all the time in jail." She smiled as I took off my shirt and slipped it on over my head. Seeing my reflection in her massive mirror I almost looked like someone else. The blouse made me seem so elegant.

"Now see, that look really works on you." Camille tilted her head sideways.

"It's a gorgeous top, but isn't it too fancy for a sober party?"

"Hmmmm... maybe, well, try this on." Camille handed me a burgundy sweater with long sleeves that went clear down to your fingertips.

When I slipped it on, I loved the feeling of being enveloped in softness.

"Now that one really flatters your body."

"It doesn't make me look too fat?"

"Girl. No...."

For the life of me, I couldn't stop stuffing the hollow place inside my face with food. I was starting to feel fat. Again. Over the next hour, I tried on a different ensemble. I hadn't realized how clothes could make you not only look different but feel different as well.

When we were done, Camille announced, "By the way, you can have these things."

"What? But you can't…."

She cut me off, "It's fine. Really. I need to clean out my closet anyway."

"Thank you so much."

A week later on the night of the party, my stomach was all tied up in knots. I didn't want to go. All my life I had prepped myself with alcohol or drugs before I went to any party, so social interactions scared me. The only problem was when I drank I would inevitably become the disaster everyone avoided.

As I arrived at the party, my heart staggered and I struggled to breathe. I pushed through feelings of wanting to run. I could hear music inside, so I went inside. There were people standing around chatting it up and sipping Perrier or Diet Coke. It felt like I had slipped into a parallel universe. I was about to turn to leave, but the hostess Chantal saw me before I could.

"Oh hi, Wendy," she smiled. "I'm so glad you were able to make it."

"Oh, hi. Ah… thanks for having me."

"Let me show you around," she said.

We weaved our way through friendly-smiling-faces to the kitchen where trays of carrots, celery, pita bread and organic hummus were all laid out on the counter top.

"We have drinks over there." Chantal pointed to a plastic tub.

Yeah. I was thirsty, but for something other than Perrier.

She disappeared and I was left on my own again. I wanted to crawl out of my skin. There was too much chatter going on in my brain. Too many people. I felt claustrophobic. My lungs felt like they might explode. I had to get away from all the people before I had a panic attack and made a fool of myself. I weaved my way into the living room with eyes darting around like a frightened animal and plopped down on a deserted sofa. As I sat there, I tried to use positive affirmations that I had been taught to calm down. *'Everything is okay, Wendy. It's just a party. No big deal.'* All of the sudden, a guy with nerdy glasses and spikey hair sat down next to me. I didn't say anything as he scanned the room.

He surprised me when he said, "These parties make me so uncomfortable.."

His words were like water, on a dry desert plains.

"They totally freak me out." I replied.

"It's all I can do to stop myself from bolting out the front door."

"Me too. Me too."

We talked for an hour and it felt good to identify the fear. Back then, I had thought I was the only one with crippling social phobia. But after that, it occurred to me that everyone might be just as scared as I was. And if that were indeed the case, perhaps if we could be honest with each other, we wouldn't feel so all alone.

The Artist's Way

I always had massive resentments towards cops. That might have been due to my encounters with them usually ended up with me being tossed in the back seat of a squad car. They were the enemy, and someone to duck and dodge, while I was using drugs. Those deeply engrained prejudices were challenged one day when a cop by the name of Justin, sat down next to me at a meeting. After we introduced ourselves, for some reason, he casually mentioned he was a police officer. My blood instantly began to boil. I almost moved seats because I didn't want to be anywhere in his jurisdiction.

What the hell is this cop doing in my meeting? He doesn't belong here.

Much to my dismay, Justin was the speaker that day. When the meeting started, he explained to everyone, how drinking was a way for police officers to unwind after being on the streets all day. I was brutally judging him up and down as he told his story. But he went on to say, that while in a blackout he got arrested for firing his service revolver out the window of his patrol car. Obviously, I related to that. His voice started to crack when he told us about waking up the next day in one of the jail cells where he worked. When I looked closer at his pale skin, tears were falling from his eyes.

What? I've never seen a cop cry before? Do they actually have emotions?

Well, it turned out that some do, and I for one was deeply touched by his vulnerability.

After the meeting we talked again. "You don't seem like other cops." I said.

"I'm not really a big fan of the 'cop' term."

"Oh, sorry, I mean, Peace Officer?" I said, with air quotes.

Although he half smiled, I could tell he was not amused.

"I really liked your share."

"Oh really? But I'm such a loser." His chin lowered to his chest.

"I was a loser before getting sober, but I just play on a different team than you."

He raised an eyebrow and gave me a sideways glance.

"Hey, do you like roller blading?" I asked.

"I love it."

"You want to go sometime?" I couldn't believe what I was saying. What had gotten into me?

"Yeah sure." He shrugged.

A few days later, Justin picked me up in his shiny new Lexus and we headed down to the beach. Once we parked, we took out our roller blading gear. I was a minimalist who only used wrist guards when I roller-bladed. Justin, on the other hand, came prepared. I waited patiently as he methodically pulled each kneepad up legs that looked like they had never seen the sun. After he put on his expensive elbow pads and wrist guards, he looked like he was wearing full body armor.

"You ready yet?" Now, I was growing impatient.

"Just need to put on my sun block is all." He said, squeezing out gobs of heavy white cream and smearing it all over his face and neck.

Then he grabbed a long-sleeved shirt, a wide-brimmed straw hat, and by the time he was ready he looked more like a farmer than a cop.

"Alright, let's go," he said.

As he skated, Justin's body was stiff and clunky. He looked like a spaz.

"How long have you been skating?" I asked.

"Oh, I've been doing it since I was a kid." He puffed out his chest.

Obviously, he had no idea how lame he looked, so I decided to show the copper how it should be done. As I picked up speed I could hear the ball bearings spinning inside my wheels as the earth rushed beneath me. My thighs and calves tightened and released while my ponytail whipped behind me in the wind. I felt like a human bullet cutting through air and space. I was unstoppable.

"HEY WAIT UP!" Justin yelled from behind.

Dropping my right skate down, I dragged it along the pavement to slow down. Then I did one of my fancy one-eighties as graceful as any Olympic skater might do.

"Wow! You're really good." Justin shook his head.

Not wanting to appear too cocky, I just smiled.

We went all the way down to Venice Beach and back again.

For some reason Justin and I seemed to click and, after that we started hanging-out together. We would go to the movies, work out or even hike, however, I still hadn't told him my whole story. That is until a month later when we were sitting at a coffee shop sipping lattes.

"You've never told me how you hit your bottom." Justin said, in an inquiring tone.

I shifted nervously in my seat. The taste of acidic shame burned at the back of my throat. I figured if told him the truth he might not want to be my friend anymore. But I knew being sober required being honest.

"Well I, I, well I had a bit of a psychotic break one night."

"A psychotic break?" One eyebrow went up.

"Well, I I, I, I sort of lost my mind."

"What does that mean?"

I took a deep breath. "Well, after days of not getting any sleep because I was doing way too much meth, I discovered my husband was cheating on me. One night, after he went to score drugs for her, I waited for them to get back. When he pulled up driving her car, I fired a couple rounds to scare the shit out of them. Unfortunately, one of the bullets hit *her*."

"Oh, my God! Was she okay?" His eyes were wide.

"Yeah… I just winged her is all."

"Thank God."

I lowered my head. "You're judging me now."

"I'm a police officer who got busted for firing his weapon within city limits. You really think I have a right to judge anyone?"

He had a point. I let out a sigh of relief.

"I suppose both of us make a good argument for gun control?"

We cracked up. It was good to laugh. I sipped my latte and when a girl came in with pink hair, it was obvious she was high on drugs.

I nodded at pinkie and said, "Do you have to restrain yourself from arresting people when you're out and about?"

"You think a plumber needs to restrain himself from fixing a broken toilet when he's out and about?"

"Well, that's different. A broken toilet isn't breaking the law."

"Look, it's what I do for a living. Arresting people is *not* a hobby of mine."

"Do you have a hobby?"

I could see his mind working behind his eyes. "Well, I've always wanted to be an artist."

"Why don't you then?"

"You know...because cops don't do art."

"Who says they don't do art?"

"They just don't. Trust me."

"You know what I've always wanted to do?"

"What?"

"I want to help people who are suffering from addiction, but I also want to write."

"So, what's stopping you?" I shrugged.

"Fear, procrastination, and laziness for starters."

He nodded as if he understood.

I had a brilliant idea.

"Why don't we do *The Artist's Way* together?"

"What's *The Artist Way*?"

"It's a workbook with a six-week plan to help someone move through their deep-seated, creative blocks."

I had been wanting to do the workbook, but wasn't good at follow through.

"Six weeks?" Justin leaned back in his chair. "Let's do it then."

The following week we met at the same coffee shop, each with our own copy of, *The Artist's Way*. We went over all the requirements in the front of the book. We would have to write three pages every day. We would need to take ourselves out on an artist date to a gallery, or a museum every week and lastly, we would discuss our progress each week.

So, each morning before work I'd get my coffee and write three pages of stream of consciousness in a spiral notepad. When I started to do this it felt like I was moving furniture around inside my head. Cleaning behind nooks and crannies, getting the old cobwebs out of my brain that I didn't realize were there.

Meanwhile, in our weekly check-in meetings I was growing fond of Justin. I found his geeky ways endearing. By the time we finished the workbook I had the onset of a crush. It was perplexing for many reasons. For one, he was a cop and I had a massive rap sheet. He was kind of square, while I was more edgy and cool.

At our end of the six weeks we were going over all the progress we had made. Justin was painting now and doing wood sculptures, and I was writing every day. We had both kept our commitments to go on the artist's dates every week. If it wasn't for his ingrained discipline from being a cop, I might not have stayed on track. I decided to confront the situation head on and lay my cards on the table, come what may.

"There's a full moon this weekend. Want to roller blade?" I asked.

Justin was game as he always was. And when the time came, Justin picked me up at five a.m. and once at the beach we put on our blades.

As we skated along the path, street lamps cast tall shadows in front of us. We rolled along until we got to the end of the bike path and sat down on a bench to take in the full moon. I shifted nervously until I mustered up the courage to talk.

"I've, been, I've been wanted to tell you something…" I stammered.

"Yeah?" he said.

"I think I'm attracted to you."

Silence. In an instant I knew I had made a huge mistake. Fuck! I began judging myself for being so vulnerable.

You must be delusional to think a cop would ever like an ex con .

Finally, he turned and said, "Look Wendy, I really like you. I do. But I don't want to complicate things because our friendship means so much to me."

I wanted to roll away on my blades, but I didn't.

"Yes. Of course, our friendship *is really* special and we wouldn't want to complicate that."

After a moment of awkwardness, I stood up. "We better get going."

After that, Justin and I talked occasionally but it wasn't the same. For a while I regretted telling him my true feelings, but eventually I realized that Justin did something for me I hadn't even expected. In hindsight, I believe Justin came into my life in order to help me heal many of my old resentments by showing me that cops were human after all.

Pixie

After doing the Artists Way, after journaling and after asking myself what I really wanted to do with my life, I ended up giving notice at the doctor's office. Several months later, I gripped a Starbucks cappuccino while riding the creaky elevator up to the sixth floor of Brotman Hospital where I was now working as a counselor in their detox center. My qualifications for the job came from my own intensive research with mind-altering substances. Who knew that my history with drugs would one day pay off? Suddenly it felt like the stars had aligned and I knew what I was put on earth to do. Change the world, one addict at a time. As the doors opened, and I got off the elevator, someone else might have thought I had entered a scene from, "The Walking Dead." But not me. The people around me were my brothers and my sisters. The ones whose lives had been downsized to a pill, a crack pipe, or a bottle of Jack Daniels. The ones who threw-up the linings of their stomachs, coming up for breath only to swear they would never drink again.

The first person I laid eyes on that morning was Taylor, who in his early twenties was just one of our many frequent fliers. He was dragging an IV pole down the hall, the corners of his hospital gown flapping while his Calvin Klein tighty-whities hung out there for everyone to see. Smiling, I just shook my head... yup, these were my peeps all right.

After checking in with the charge nurse, I grabbed a couple of oversized vinyl charts and headed for the office that I shared with Joe, the male counselor on the unit. Sitting down, I dove into my paperwork, and with my reading glasses on, I appeared more like a medical doctor than the ex-junkie that I actually was.

"Buenos Dias," Joe said, as he swaggered in.

"You're late again, Jose."

"Well, I guess I haven't transcended humanity like you have, Wendy," he replied.

Thrusting my middle finger in his direction, he started to laugh. Joe was a Hispanic, ex-punk rocker with arms covered in a web-work of intricate tattoos that extended from his wrist to his neck. We were two sober soldiers on the front lines. Joe and I witnessed things most people don't see in their entire lives. A lot of our patients wouldn't make it. In fact, we averaged about one death a month and those were just the clients that we knew about. There were the others who went MIA, and when addicts go missing, it's usually not a good thing.

By ten o'clock it was time for morning process group and within minutes all the seats in the circle were full. Joe settled in on one side and I sat across from him.

"Okay, you guys it's check-in time! Please give one word that best describes how you feel?" I said, nodding to the stringy-haired girl with trashy clothes on my left.

As she stared at the ceiling contemplating her current emotional temperature, I could tell she was a tweaker, a term used for meth heads for their unique ability to stay awake for 'two weeks' straight.

The door flung open and everyone turned to watch as a young pixie-looking girl with delicate features came in late. It took her a moment but after she found a seat, I resumed the group.

"One word," I said.

"Annoyed," the tweaker replied, slumping down in her chair.

Using my active listening skills, I nodded my head before moving on to the next patient. When it was Pixie's turn, she whispered softly, "I'm scared." Having struck a chord, everyone in the group nodded. When we had gone around the entire circle, I opened it up for anyone who had a burning desire to share.

After an hour, group was over and the patients headed outside for a cigarette break while I asked to meet with Pixie.

"I'm going to be your counselor while you are here," I told her, as she sat down at my desk. She shrugged, staring blankly at the floor.

"What are you kicking?"

"Klonopin."

Klonopin, a sedative that is prescribed for anxiety, can sometimes cause side effects such as blinding headaches, confusion, hallucinations, increased panic, and thoughts of harming oneself, to name a few.

"Do you want to get off them?"

"I do... but I don't know if I can."

"Yeah, that's how I felt alright."

"You were on them?" she asked, her brow creased like a paper fan.

"A long, long time ago."

"Was it hard coming off?"

Not wanting to discourage her, I didn't tell her that while kicking cold turkey in jail my joints had seized-up like uncoiled pistons and my flesh had crawled with the sensation of a thousand invisible bugs. I also didn't mention the seizures, or how I was eventually rushed to the hospital in an ambulance to be revived. Instead, I calmly said it wasn't easy but I was grateful to be on the other side.

She studied me for a moment, her mind working behind her eyes. She wanted to believe me. I could tell.

Unfortunately, within days Pixie was in the throes of one of the worst detoxes I had ever seen. Each morning when I got off the elevator Pixie would be there waiting for me, her skin glistening with sweat.

"I can't do this anymore," she whined.

For Pixie, it wasn't one day at a time. It was an hour, a minute, and a second at a time. "Maybe I should just stay on the Klonopin?"

"They weren't working for you anymore, remember Sweetie?"

Every day for the next few weeks Pixie paced the long hallway like a feral cat. Periodically she'd peek into my office and if I was free she'd come in and sit down, looking up from her incredibly sad almond eyes.

"I want to crawl in a hole and die," she said.

I knew down in the marrow of my bones what that felt like. And although at times I wanted to forget, I knew it was the broken places in me that could help her.

"Yeah, I remember feeling like that."

She paused and let out a long sigh.

"You're the only one who knows what this is like."

"And I promise you girl... IT WILL PASS."

Pixie reminded me what it used to be like, in a way no one else had before. Psychologists call it counter-transference when you deeply relate to a patient that you are seeing in a professional capacity. All I know was Pixie had pierced through my internal boundaries and wormed her way right into my heart. After six grueling weeks of what I can only equate with torture, she was finally off those fucking pills. I couldn't have been more proud of her if she were my own daughter graduating college with honors. Before her release date from the hospital, I sat down with her once again.

"You need to go somewhere to get stronger." Without giving me any fight, Pixie agreed and I was able to call around and find her a respected, long-term treatment center nearby. On her discharge day she came into my office, dressed in Levi's and a pale blue hoodie.

"I just wanted to say good-bye," she said, with a quivering smile. "You know I couldn't have done it without you."

"Just do me a favor girl, and don't do any more pills again?"

"No, never again." She shook her head fiercely.

"Can I call you when I need to do a feeling check-in?"

"Sure," I said. "I might even let you use more than one word."

When we hugged, a golf ball-size lump formed in the back of my throat. I swallowed it down hard and waved as Pixie rolled her suitcase behind her, leaving my office for the last time.

Several months later I was buried in my paperwork when Joe came to my desk with a somber look on his face.

"What's wrong?" I asked, leaning back.

"I just got a call from Pixie's treatment center. She took a handful of pills when her father was flying in for a visit and collapsed at the airport. She died on the way to the hospital."

My stomach coiled in on itself. Pixie had gone through hell. I just assumed she would be one of the ones that would go on to make it.

Sober, it felt as if the tectonic plates shifted and shot me deep into a dark abyss. I rushed to the bathroom where tears fell by the fistfuls. Without my usual shock absorbers, I felt everything.

While I never learned why Pixie killed herself, what I did learn was that while I may be able to carry the message, no matter how hard I try, I will never be able to carry the addict. For me, getting sober was the hardest thing I'd ever done. It was like going through the eye of the needle. For all of us that do make it to the other side, it will always remain an inside job.

Full Circle

B uddy, a scruffy, bearded guy, who I'd seen in meetings, was always trying to get people to go with him to feed the homeless on Skid Row. One day he approached me with one of his noble causes.

"Can you go to a men's prison with a few of us to tell your story?" he asked.

Members of twelve-step meetings often take panels into jails, prisons and hospitals to share their experience on how they got sober. I wanted to be of service, so I said yes even though public speaking scared me to death.

On the day of the panel, we crawled along in rush hour traffic. There were four of us; Buddy who was driving, Joe, a surfer dude sitting shot gun and Rosie, a blond rocker chick in the back of the van with me.

"I can't believe I'm going to men's prison on Valentine's Day." Rosie shook her head. "I've been sober nine months and I thought surely I'd have a boyfriend by now."

Surfer Joe looked over at Buddy and rolled his eyes.

Rosie lowered her voice. "Look at us. We are two hot chicks and we should have guys bringing us flowers and taking us out for romantic dinners." She looked up to the heavens like she was expecting to get an answer right there. I didn't feel like a hot chick at all.

An hour later we got off the freeway in the middle of shit-kicking country. The van jig-sawed through the back roads passing brown fields and cattle farms dotted with green. My throat closed as the scent of manure seeped in through the air vents. Ten minutes later we were driving alongside the gates of Chino Correctional Facility that could have easily been mistaken for a military base if it weren't for the two high fences with looped razor wire that ran along its perimeter. Beyond that were rows of drab green barracks with the American flag flying from a pole.

My stomach churned as the van rolled to a stop in the parking lot. "Alright guys, leave everything here except your I.D.'s. No purses or keys in your pockets or you're more likely to get searched." Rosie and I hoped out the side door until Buddy joined us with a pink box of donuts.

"What are we supposed to talk about, Buddy?" I thought maybe if I had more information I wouldn't be so nervous.

"All you have to do is talk about what it was like, what happened and what it's like now."

"But I'm not good at public speaking," I replied.

"You'll have a captive audience, so don't worry." Buddy winked at Surfer Joe and they both laughed out loud.

"You better not make me go first, is all I can say," I snapped back.

"No problem."

We walked across the parking lot and made our way to the reflective glass door and entered the main lobby. A correctional officer with a closed-cropped military cut sat behind a thick, bullet-proof glass. His eyes narrowed until you could tell he recognized Buddy, who bent over to speak through the metal grid. "How's it going?" he said to the officer.

"Whatcha got for us tonight, pal?"

"Brought a Valentine's Day panel for the guys."

"I'll need to see everyone's driver's licenses."

Everyone slipped their laminated I.D.'s into a slit at the bottom of the quarter-inch glass. The officer compared the pictures on the I.D. card to our faces. When satisfied we weren't impostors, he said, "Have a seat until I can get somebody out here to take you back."

"Thanks." Buddy waved.

We sat down on hard plastic chairs. Ten minutes passed in silence when a tall, stern-faced guard opened the side door. "Ya' all can come with me," he said.

We entered into a cold corridor and when the door slammed shut behind us, I flinched. The hollow sound of the lock slipping into place made my knees go weak. I was flooded with memories of the last time I went to jail. How did I get from being a woman running down the street with a .38 to someone who voluntarily goes into a men's prison to talk? It almost felt like I had been plucked from one life and dropped into another.

The sound of the officer's shiny boots echoed through the long corridor as we followed behind him. Finally, we came to another door where he slid in his key and let us outside. I squinted against the multiple searchlights that lit up every inch of the yard.

Rosie grabbed my arm. "Oh my God, we are actually inside a men's prison."

"Surreal," was all I managed to say.

Walking shoulder-to-shoulder we came to a chain-linked enclosure that had workout benches, barbells and scattered jump ropes arranged on a thick, black tarmac. Inside the enclosure were a dozen glistening men who had been working out, but when they saw us they looked up. "Well, hellooooo ladieeees," someone said.

"Holy shit, would you look at all those bodies?" Rosie whispered.

We linked arms and giggled like two adolescent schoolgirls.

"You two might end up finding a boyfriend after all," Surfer Joe teased.

We gazed at the half-naked men whose muscles were so tight they looked like they could rip right through their bulging, tattooed skins. They glared at us as we walked down the path to a classroom where inmates stood talking in small groups. A Latino guy with khaki pants clear to his chest stood in the corner. A bald white guy with a ponytail and a wiry goatee stood with thick, tattooed arms crossed in front of his chest. He looked us up and down. In the back of the room was a beefy officer in a black SWAT-style uniform, keeping an eye on everything.

"Oh, my fucking god," Rosie said through tight ventriloquist lips.

It was jarring to be without a fence or wall to hold the men back. I'm sure they hadn't had sex for a while and I knew it would take more than one officer to stop all these men from rushing us if they wanted to get it on. My heart thumped against my chest. I shifted nervously in place. The air smelled of too much cologne.

A young kid with unkempt hair and bright blue eyes rushed over to greet us. He had an innocence that made it seem like he wouldn't be capable of committing any crime. On the front of his orange jumper was the word TRUSTEE in bold black letters. He stretched out his hand. "Welcome ladies."

"Thanks," Rosie and I answered in unison.

Buddy held out the box of donuts as an offering. "Can you put these out for the guys?"

"No problem." Baby Face was eager to help.

Buddy directed us to fold-out chairs in the front of the room. The cold metal sent a shiver clear up my spine when I sat down.

Buddy cupped his hands around his mouth. "Hey guys! We're going to get started now."

Eventually, the men settled into the rows of chairs facing us just a few feet away. I accidentally locked eyes with a Hispanic kid and averted my gaze. Fuck! It was almost like I could see the accumulation of all his pain staring at me. A lot of them had dark circles under their eyes and looked stressed out. I figured it must be the prison life, which can be twice as bad if you happen to be a man. I shifted toward the other panelists so I wouldn't have to look anyone directly in the eye.

Buddy started the introduction. "Hey guys, I brought some people from A.A to share their experiences with you. In fact, on our drive over here this evening, the girls were saying there was no other place they'd rather be on Valentine's Day than here."

I wanted to throw a donut at Buddy's head.

"Our first speaker this evening is the lovely Rosie."

When Rosie started, I barely heard a thing she said. The ceiling fan turned slowly up above. I was totally in my own head thinking about my favorite subject, me. What would I say? But then Rosie started talking about a fight she'd had with an ex-boyfriend before she got clean. "He was yelling at me for drinking too much. I was sick of his shit, so I threw myself out of the car onto the freeway. Don't ask me how, but I ended-up on the side of the freeway without even breaking a bone. When the paramedics got there, they took me to the hospital where I was put on a hold for being a danger to myself."

"That's called a 5150, girl," a gravelly voice in the back said.

Rosie shook her head as she recalled a darker time in her life. "Yup, I'm a nurse so I know what a 5150 is. But the next day, when I saw the psychiatrist I told him I was just having a fight with my boyfriend and that's why I did what I did. He must have thought I was out of my mind."

It was hard to imagine the pretty girl sitting next to me could do such crazy things but I was well aware that some of us clean up really good.

She went on to say. "What a relief to find out I was an alcoholic and not crazy after all." The room erupted in laughter. "I've been going to meetings every day since I got out of the hospital and I haven't had a drink for over a year."

The men applauded and a couple of them even whistled their praise. It was time for Surfer Joe to speak and then it became my turn. My insides were shaky with fear. As much as I wanted to be dazzling and brilliant, I stumbled over my words. At one point I realized, I was talking way too fast and stopped mid-sentence staring at the floor. I could feel the men glaring at me as I squirmed nervously in my seat. My chest heaved. I took a breath and tried again. "I, I was asking myself today what I could say that could make a difference when you guys go back to your bunks tonight? And all I can tell you is what it was like for me."

As I talked, the blurry parts of my life began to take form. I told the men about my mother's suicide, and how her stuff started to disappear from the house after her death. First it was her clothes, then her collection of ceramic cats, and eventually the pictures of her came down off the walls. I told the men that I was cobbled together by disappointment, broken promises, secrets and lies, and how I used this as evidence in my airtight case against there being any sort of God. I became angry. I turned that anger inward until it grew into a beast.

"I blamed everyone else for my life. It was my mother's fault, my father's fault, and later, it would be my husband's fault. Until eventually, I ended up in jail on assault with a deadly weapon charges and finally, I realized it wasn't them who was to blame. I was the one common denominator to all my problems. If I wanted my life to be different I would have to change."

When the meeting was all over, some of the men came up, to thank us. They were so gracious and real it touched my heart. I noticed the Cholo dude with the tattoos on his neck hanging back at the end of the line. He was the last one to talk to me and I will never forget what he said.

"I've never heard my story told before. My mother was crazy and killed herself when I was kid. Over time I just became angry at the world."

"I know what that's like." I shook my head.

"But, but have you really forgiven her?" he asked.

"Forgiving my mother meant I was free to start living my own life instead of living hers."

I could see his mind working behind sad brown eyes. "Well, that is something I certainly will take back to my bunk tonight." And he turned and walked away.

School of Hard Knocks

One afternoon while working at the detox, the nurse told me Rikki was on the phone. Since he never called, I knew instantly something was up. My heart leapt to my throat as I snatched up the receiver. "Rikki? What's wrong?"

"Mom, my front tooth got knocked out and the other one is hanging loose."

"Wha, what happened?"

"A guy elbowed me on the basketball court." His voice cracked.

Rikki went to the Boys and Girls Club after school to play ball.

"Did you tell any of the staff?"

"No. I, I, I ran home...Mom, please hurry..."

My stomach was clenched in a fist. This was my biggest and most pressing fear. I was always scared something bad would happen if I wasn't there. A penalty for being a single mother for sure. A haziness wrapped itself around my head. I blinked a couple times trying to right my center of gravity. "I'll be right there." I said, slamming down the phone.

I grabbed my purse, explained to the charge nurse that I had an emergency at home, and rushed for the elevator. Once outside I had to squint against the brightness of the sun. My pumps clicked against the pavement as I ran across the parking lot. When I got to my car I was completely out of breath. I turned the ignition and threw the car into reverse. The tires screeched as I took off. My fingers gripped the steering wheel while my thoughts pinged like a pinball machine inside my head. What the hell am I going to do? Go to the ER? To the dentist? Maybe I should take him to urgent care? Sweat dripped down the center of my back.

As I weaved my way through traffic there was a dull throbbing behind my eyes. My frantic thoughts kept repeating like a CD stuck on skip-repeat. A narrow loop that kept telling me that whatever I was walking into would be way too much to handle. It would seem that without any stability growing up, I was prone to becoming hysterical when something unexpected happened to my kids. I sank deeper into the black hole known as my mind. I was driving when I caught sight of the sticker on my dashboard. My latest mantra, *everything is all right*. I turned off the radio and chanted it inside the car. "Everything is all right. Everything is all right. Everything is all right." I must have said it a hundred times in an effort to quiet the committee inside my brain.

When I got home, I parked the car, bolted up the steps and flung the front door open. A sickening shiver ran through me as Rikki stood with his front tooth, root and all, in the middle of his palm. His eyes look horrified. It took my breath away. When Rikki lifted his upper lip, he exposed a hole that looked like a blacked-out window of an abandoned building. The other front tooth was dislodged and hanging loosely by a thread. The blood rushed to my face. This was where I typically would fall apart but, I caught myself and said, "Everything is going to be alright Rikki." There was a forced calm in my voice that surprised even me. His shoulders seemed to soften from around his ears. His chest heaved as he took a deep breath. His brown almond eyes studied me a moment so, I said it again. "Everything is going to be alright." I stepped closer and folded him in my arms, "We will get it fixed no matter what it takes. I promise."

"But how?"

"Dr. Little will know what to do."

Only because I was sober, I had recently found a dentist whom Rikki really liked.

Ten minutes later we were standing at the reception desk in Dr. Little's lobby.

"I have an emergency," I said.

The dark-haired receptionist looked up at Rikki, who was holding the bloody towel over his mouth. "Let me find an empty room." Her voice was laced with concern.

We were quickly ushered into an exam room where Rikki was directed to get into the over-sized chair. A young, blond dental assistant in blue scrubs, and a ponytail came in and started cleaning up the blood. Rikki glared at me over the assistant's shoulder the entire time.

Moments later, Dr. Little rushed into the room with his cheeks flushed. "Hey young man, I heard you had a bit of an accident?"

Rikki held out the tooth still in his hand.

"Let's put that in some water." Dr. Little carefully picked it up and handed it to his assistant.

"Let me see what's going on in there." Dr. Little lifted the top lip like a curtain and shined a small penlight inside. "You're definitely going to need some stitches, young man."

"Do you think you can save the tooth, Dr. Little?" I asked from behind.

Dr. Little turned around. "I'm going to try, but sometimes if a tooth has been out too long it dies. He can always get an implant if it doesn't take. But for now, I'm going to try and put it back in."

"Should I stay?" I looked at Rikki, then Dr. Little, and back at Rikki.

"It would be better if you wait in the lobby. This might take a little while."

"Rikki are you okay?"

"Yeah... I'll be okay."

"I love you..." I said, before I left.

I passed through the lobby and out the front door. My throat squeezed in on itself. My knees felt weak as I leaned against the wall for support, and tears filled my eyes. Since there weren't any self-help books for Jail-Bird Moms I was probably getting the best on-the-job training one could ever hope for just by showing up.

A Family Disease

After cycling through prison a couple more times Jerry finally stopped doing hard drugs when he realized that he was wasting his life. After that, he married his pretty blond girlfriend, Erika, and they started having kids of their own. Several years later, they had two boys and two girls and Erika and Jerry seemed committed to give them a good life. Jerry got a truck driver job and saved enough money to buy a home in Riverside, an hour east of LA.

As my children began to thrive much of the guilt I carried for being an absent parent began to recede. However, that bubble burst when Jerry came over, sat down on the couch, cupping his face in his hands. A familiar surge of adrenaline rushed through me when I realized something was wrong.

"Erika is using again," he said.

I sat down beside him. "But I thought you guys had stopped a long time ago?"

"She's doing it behind my back."

I was livid. *How could she do this?* Erika was disrupting my hard earned peace of mind.

With very little tolerance at this point, I suggested, "Maybe you should get a divorce."

"Mom, I love her. I'm not going to leave her," he snapped.

"Okay. Okay. I get it. Then what's the plan?"

"Can you please help her?"

Ever since I got my counseling credentials people acted like I had some sort of magical powers that I could use to get addicts clean and sober. That somehow I could access compliance when no one else could. While I knew more than anyone that willingness was an inside job, I told my son I would try to help.

After making a few phone calls the next day, I found Erika a sober living house and an outpatient program where she could work on herself. I called Jerry and told him the good news.

"Can you tell her she needs to go, Mom?" he pleaded.

"Put her on the phone." I said, with a fierce determination.

When I told Erika the plan, I was surprised that she was not on board.

"Thanks, but I've just decided to go to meetings."

"But didn't you say that last time you stopped?"

"This time I'll do it. I promise."

I didn't press on any further. I was powerless and knew it was entirely up to her.

A month passed, when my phone rang again with Erika sobbing in a state of hysterics.

"Slow down, I can't understand what you're saying." I tried to maintain some semblance of calm.

"Jerry said he's going to leave me."

"What the hell happened this time?" I white-knuckled that receiver in my hand.

"I started using again Wendy," she sobbed.

"I thought you were going to meetings?"

"I didn't have time to go."

I talked her off the edge and again, she promised to get some help.

When I got off the phone I was livid. I paced back and forth in my living room.

How can she be doing this now when everyone else is doing good? This is unacceptable. It needs to stop.

Later that night while lying in bed I couldn't sleep. I was worried and wanted everybody in the family to be alright. I bounced ideas around in my head trying to think of a way to 'fix' the problem. And in my mind, Erika was the problem. It was her behaviors that were causing havoc within the family system. All of the sudden I had a chilling realization.

Oh my God. Jerry has married his mother. Erika is me.

the thought made the bones want to drop straight out of my flesh.

Had I become so insulated with my thriving sober life that I forgot what would happen when I did drugs? Or was Erika holding up a mirror that gave me the unique experience of feeling the pain of being on the receiving end of another's addiction? It was like getting a slap in the face. Clearly, the tables had turned.

When I looked back at my own addiction, I remembered how Jennie, my own mother-in-law, was the one who stood by me and my children, praying countless rosaries to save my lost soul.

So why then was I so ready to throw in the towel with Erika?

That's when it occurred to me, if I couldn't forgive Erika for her addiction, I would never be able to forgive myself for mine. So, just like Jennie had prayed for me, I started to pray for Erika. Only, I didn't say the rosary and instead I asked Jennie, who had recently passed away, if she could do anything from the other side of the veil to please, please, please, help Erika get clean.

I'm not sure how much time passed, but one day I got a call from Erika. I braced myself for more bad news.

"I'm done," she said. "I can't do it anymore."

"What do you mean?"

"I'm not going to use anymore. I hate who I've become."

I let out a long sigh. Part of me wanted to believe her, but another part of me was skeptical. But as the days, weeks and months went by, it became evident that Erika was committed to staying clean. I watched in awe as she transformed herself into a loving mother, a devoted wife and a respectful woman. It was amazing to witness the enormous strides that she made in that first year. It seemed, once again, that prayers had worked, or at least, that's what I choose to believe.

Self-Care

I was at work at the detox center when I leaned over to pick something up and felt a sharp, painful, pinch in my lower back. When I tried to stand erect I couldn't get back up. It was so intense it made my insides scream.

I was holding the edge of my desk when Joe, my work co-hort strutted in.

"Have you been drinking again Wendy?" he laughed.

"My back has gone out."

"Oh dear, I'm sorry. You okay?" There was a sudden concern in his voice.

"It hurts."

"You better go home."

I tilted my head to look at him. "But my clients."

"Don't worry. I can handle things around here."

Self-care was not a word even in my vocabulary until I got sober. Who takes care of themselves when you're using drugs? Not me. And while I had started talking about self-care to clients, it was harder to implement into my life. Sure, I could get a pedicure or do my hair and I even had a massage once in a while, but to really put myself first was something I hadn't learned how to do yet.

Besides, I loved my job to the point that my work ethic bordered on madness. I thought I couldn't lose any time with a client. They were there for such a short time before their insurance ran out for medical detox benefits. It was my job to convince them to go onto residential treatment or outpatient care, which their insurance would pay for. The more time you can keep an addict away from their old life style, the more it increases the odds of them staying sober. But the pain gripped me and I couldn't listen to clients with a face pinched in agony.

"Alright, alright. Only if you check in with all my clients." I moved slowly around my desk, and grabbed my purse.

"I'll help you get to your car."

Joe held my arm and led me to the elevator. It felt like my knees might buckle. When we got outside, the sun slapped me in the face with its brightness. I shuffled like an eighty-year-old geriatric patient.

"Maybe you should go to the doctor," he said, as we approached my car.

"I don't have a doctor."

I had health insurance, but doctors had always been a vehicle for me to get prescriptions. When I was using I wanted their pills. Any kind of pills, but mostly opiates and benzos. Meth may have brought me to my knees but my drug of choice, hands down, was opiates. I liked them because opiates gave me a pharmaceutical embrace on the inside. They quieted my mind and relaxed every cell in the body. I knew I had to stay away from them if I wanted to stay sober. Unless, I went under the knife, otherwise, they were off limits.

"You need to see someone," Joe said, as he helped me in my car.

I nodded. "Alright, alright…I will…and thanks for the help."

I don't know how people function in pain. If you felt like an ice pick was stabbing your body, why wouldn't you turn to pain meds? Just pressing on the gas pedal caused me searing pain up my spine. When I got home, I took the steps one at a time while holding onto the iron rail and pulling myself up to the next stair. Rikki was still at school, so I was on my own.

Once inside my apartment, I dropped my purse on the floor and went for the Advil, popping four in my mouth at once. Afterwards, I slowly lowered myself onto the coach to wait for any signs of relief.

I'd been self-sufficient for so long that I sometimes didn't know when to ask for help. This was not one of those times. I needed to see a doctor even if they were a trigger for me. I pushed myself up and got the phone book that felt like it weighed a thousand pounds. These were the days before Google and Yelp where you'd have to search the yellow pages. I wanted a woman doctor, and someone who was open to alternative medicine. I didn't want to jeopardize my precious sobriety by going up against a physician who was aligned with Big Pharma and pushing drugs.

My finger went over names and stopped when it came to Dr. Barnaby. She was a little over a mile away, and the small ad said she was an integrative MD. I liked the sound of that, so I picked up the phone and called the number.

"Dr. Barnaby's office. How can I help you?"

"I need to see the doctor."

"Are you a new patient?"

"Yes."

"Our first opening is in two weeks."

"I can't wait. I'm in pain now."

"Oh. What kind of pain?"

"My back went out."

"Hold on please." A good five minutes went by before she picked up again. "She can squeeze you in after lunch."

"Thank you. I'll be there."

I don't remember going to their office. I don't remember checking-in with the receptionist but I do remember having way too many forms to fill out. I remember a nurse in floral scrubs stood at the door and called my name. I pushed myself up and went to the exam room.

"Let's get your weight," she said, standing in front of the scale. I could barely lift my feet up onto the platform. An animal sound escaped my lips when I almost slipped. The all-consuming pain radiated inside me like a scream.

"You okay honey?"

"No." I shook my head.

"Why don't you get up on the exam table and lay down."

I managed to crawl up on the tissue-covered exam table and lowered myself down.

"Try to relax and the doctor will be in in a minute." She slipped out the door.

I opened my eyes a few minutes later to Dr. Barnaby who had red hair, freckles and a halo of concern on her face. "I hear you're back went out?" she said.

"I've never felt such pain in my life." I pushed myself up.

She sat down on a stool and inquired on my medical history. Annoyed at the line of questioning, I must have grunted my answers. I didn't want to go over my parents' history. I just wanted immediate relief. I was grateful when Dr. Barnaby was finished and ordered the nurse to give me a shot of Flexeril, a muscle relaxant that was non-addictive.

"Come to my office after you get your shot," the doctor said before she left.

Moments later, I watched the nurse draw up clear liquid from a vial into a tubular syringe. My mind raced back to my early twenties when I was an IV user. I definitely had a needle fetish back then. Most junkies do. The mere sight of a syringe could trigger cravings so intense it could send you looking for a dealer in McArthur Park to score. Not taking any chances, I looked the other way.

"This may stick a little," the nurse said leaning behind me.

There was the prick of the needle in my buttocks and within seconds I could feel the sweet release of my muscles. The nurse dabbed me with alcohol and I pulled my pants up. I was walking better, but no surprise there. Medications always did the trick for me.

Moments later, the nurse escorted me down a short hall to the doctor's office. It was decorated with rows of medical books. Ah, yes. How many doctors' offices like this had I been in pleading a case for anxiety meds, opiates to make me feel better? How many quacks had scribbled out a prescription for Valiums or Vicodin with multiple refills? It was so easy back then to get anything, even if I was seeking relief from the emotional pain. But sober, I wasn't taking any chances, but there had to be something to alleviate pain that would not jeopardize my sobriety.

"Have a seat," Dr. Barnaby said.

Slowly, I lowered myself into a chair that sat on the other side of her desk.

"Better?"

"Yes. That helped a lot."

She nodded and a strand of red hair fell across her freckled cheek. "You seem to have a pinched nerve causing back spasms. It can be very painful, but usually goes away with rest within a week. Meanwhile, I can write you a prescription for Vicodin to help…."

I shook my head fiercely. "I can't take Vicodin."

"You're allergic?"

"It's more like I used to be a heroin addict."

"Oh. I can give you Ultram then. It's what I give to all my sober patients."

I was relieved that she saw other sober people. My internal guard went down and then I asked, "What is Ultram?"

"It's a non-addictive pain medication. It's very safe."

She scribbled on her prescription pad and slid it across her desk. When I picked it up, I studied the directions. One pill every six hours as needed for pain. Why hadn't I heard of this drug before? I noticed a pocket-sized PDR, which is basically a pharmaceutical guide, sitting on her desk. I used to have my own PDR back in the day and studied it to learn what drugs got you high.

"Can we get the breakdown of Ultram in your PDR?"

"Sure. If you like."

"Yup. I think it would."

Dr. Barnaby started flipping through the flimsy-tissue pages. When she found Ultram, she started reading out loud. "Ultram is used to relieve moderate to moderately severe pain in people who need it around the clock." She read on, blah, blah, blah but my ears perked up when she said, "Do not prescribe Ultram to patients who have depression or addiction problems, such as patients with alcoholism." Her brow creased like a paper fan. "I don't know why I didn't see that before," she said.

I pushed the prescription across the desk.

"I'm so sorry."

"Can you give me some extra strength Motrin instead?"

"Of course." Her face was flushed as she wrote another script.

I am not against taking something when you're in severe pain but this was manageable pain. The Motrin worked. What I learned was that doctors don't know what a person has to go through to get sober. She didn't know how I struggled for years. That I went to jails, lost a husband, hurt my kids, stole, lied to escape reality. Doctors aren't supposed to know all that. It's not their job. But sobriety is not a low hanging fruit that you pick off the bottom of the tree. It takes work. And it turns out, I have a healthy streak of paranoia, that if I'm not vigilant, I could end up using again or going back to jail.

The Relapse

It was the summer of 2012 when I got a call from Jerry. He was out of breath. "Dad's in Torrance Hospital. I'm going down there to see him now," he said.

My heart hammered inside my chest. "What the hell happened?" I asked.

"Lisa called and said he had a heart attack."

Max was sixty-years-old but he'd never had heart problems before. "I'll get Rikki and we'll see you down there."

I hadn't talked to Max for months. There was no need to, considering we had both gone our separate ways. Honestly, I was relieved to have moved on from him. We had nothing in common and when I did see him, I knew I would be filled with regret for all the years I'd wasted with him. But he was the father of my boys and I felt like I needed to be there in case he didn't make it.

It seemed odd that we were going to a hospital to see Max, considering how he had survived so many close calls back when we were using heroin. I started thinking about how hard and how long I had loved him. I had been codependent. As his wife I became the incredible shrinking woman. But things were different now. I had not only moved on, I was thriving. I had meaningful friendships. I traveled. I was making good money as the director of an out-patient center. More importantly, I had formed my own ideas, beliefs and goals and no longer deferred to my man's point of view. To think I could have bumped along as his bitter and unhappy wife for the rest of my day's if I hadn't gone to jail. Sometimes a seemingly bad thing can turn out to be a good thing in disguise.

Thirty minutes later, Rikki and I arrived at the hospital. We jumped out of the car and headed toward the Emergency Room. I heard someone yell, "Mom!" I turned around and

Jerry was rushing towards us. We exchanged hugs and continued walking. We were just about to enter the emergency room
when we were greeted by Max's mother-in-law, who had perfectly coifed silver hair and a Gucci bag dangling from her arm.
"I'm afraid your Dad isn't doing well," she said.

"What happened?" Jerry asked.

"He's on life support. I don't know if he'll make it through
the night."

My mind looked for reasons as to why this was happening.
He didn't eat right. He was a couch potato. He had never learned
how to take care of himself. I thought surely, that would have
never happened if I had still been his wife.

"My Dad will make it," Jerry said with such force it brought
me back to the moment.

Just then, Lisa came rushing through the automatic glass
doors. She appeared thinner, her hair disheveled, and she had
dark rings under her eyes. When she saw me, her chest expanded
as she took in a deep breath. Lisa had always felt insecure around
me, I could tell. It may have been because I was the ex-wife who
had shot the other woman, but it may have been just who she
was.

"What happened to my Dad?" Jerry asked.

"Ah, I, well I found Max on the floor this morning… when
I shook him he wouldn't wake up." Her eyes darted around. "I, I
didn't know what to do. I thought he'd fainted but he had had a
heart attack…" Pools of tears filled her eyes.

Her mother pulled out a tissue from the Gucci bag and
handed one to her.

"Lisa, do you mind if I go in to see Max with the boys?" I
said.

Lisa looked at Jerry and Rikki as if she were seeing them for
the first time. "Yes. Of course. Of course." She waved her hand.

With a taut nod of my head, my boys and I walked inside
where we got name tags and masks so we wouldn't transmit any
germs. The security doors released and the three of us walked

down a long corridor. We passed nurses in blue scrubs rushing about. The P.A. system blared overhead, but couldn't penetrate the chatter inside my head. I was wondering what my role was in all of this? What do I do when the boys see their father? Unconscious, would he be able to hear them? I took a deep breath and tried to calm myself down.

When we found the room number, I pushed open the door. I heard the constant beep, beep, beep of the heart monitor. My breath caught in the back of my throat. I stared at Max who was gray, with a tube running out of his mouth and needles in the back of his hand leading to an IV bag hanging on a pole. A pulse monitor was clipped to his index finger. The smell of disinfectant hung in the air and intrusively seeped through my mask.

Jerry circled to the other side of the bed and closely examined his father's face. Rikki was at the foot of the bed. An icy chill ran up my spine. A sadness started to rise up inside me. I grew up with this man. We had spent years together. He had once been my everything and now he was teetering on the edge of death.

A bewildered Rikki looked at me. All I could do was hold a hand over my heart and shake my head. When I looked across at Jerry, he was gripping his hands over the top of his shaved head. Seeing his dad on life support seemed too much for him. He made his way around the bed and pushed the door open. Rikki and I followed him. Once in the lobby, Jerry leaned his back against the wall, bent over and puts his hand on his knees. He sobbed. The toughest of my sons had always been the more emotional one. I draped an arm across his back. "It's okay. It's okay." I tried to comfort him.

"What if he dies?"

I talked slowly to make sure he heard me. "Right. Now. Your. Dad. Is. Alive. We don't know what's going to happen yet."

"Why don't we go outside and get some fresh air?" Rikki said, the voice of reason.

With his face flushed, Jerry pushed himself up and turned toward the exit. We followed behind. Stepping outside, the sun slapped me in my face. Lisa was still there with her mom. For a moment no one said anything. We just stood there. It was like all the oxygen was pulled from us and left back in that hospital room.

Until Jerry asked, "What are the doctors saying about my dad?"

Lisa was biting the orange nail polish off her nails. "One doctor asked me if he was doing any drugs."

I stepped in closer. "Isn't Max sober?"

"Well, yes but he's been taking something for back pain."

"What was he taking?"

"Methadone…."

"Methadone? For back pain?"

"Yes. It was chronic pain but he had stopped taking it a while ago…"

Lisa was shifting on her feet like a nervous terrier. Her mother stood behind her, eyes cast down. My stellar bullshit detector knew Lisa was withholding information. I was already peeling back the layers of deception in my mind. Something was not right and I felt it in my gut. I could pry, and try to get more answers but I wasn't there to be a detective, a role that comes easily for me. I was there to be an anchor for my boys, not some Sherlock Holmes.

For the first few days it was touch and go. No one was sure if Max would pull through. By the third day, there was talk that if Max did wake-up he might have brain damage. I was bracing myself for the phone call but it never came. Instead, a week later, Jerry called me telling me his Dad had regained consciousness. I decided to go see him again. When I arrived in the ICU, Max was sitting up and sipping on apple juice and Lisa had gone to the cafeteria. When he saw me, he lowered his head and set down the juice. His lower lip began to quiver. "I lost my sixteen years," he cried.

Silence.

"What happened?" I asked.

"I did some heroin... and I guess I did too much."

For a long time, I had resented this man for trading me in for a younger woman. Oh sure, we had made amends, but I still some residual resentments. All I knew was, that if any cell in my body had come there to judge, it was gone. I knew I was no better than him and it could be me in that hospital bed. Or, I could have been the wife having to take care of him, but fortunately, neither of those things were true. Seeing Max's close encounter with death moved me a step closer to letting go of the past. When I placed my hand on his trembling shoulder, I wasn't showing up as his wife, I was showing up as his friend.

Amends

My first sponsor once told me, "You're going to have to make amends to all the people you've harmed," she said.

"What if I just take out an ad in the LA Times and apologize to everyone I ever hurt?" I said.

"I'm supposed to make amends to Cat?"

"Especially to Cat."

"But why should I be the one to apologize? She's the home-wrecking bitch who stole my old man."

"Maybe because you shot her?"

"But I, I …"

"You could have left him anytime."

"I didn't know that back then."

I wasn't ready to make amends yet and my sponsor and I went our separate ways. Five years later I was with another sponsor, Julie who had long wavy black hair and rectangle glasses.

"I'm wondering if I should just bite the bullet and make amends to Cat?" I said.

"Not sure if biting the bullet is the best term to use?"

"Yeah. Guess you're right."

We laughed.

"But how would I do it?"

"What was your part in all of it."

I pinched the bridge of my nose. "Shooting her?" I looked up.

"Ya think?"

"But what do I say?"

"Just own your part and apologize for it."

I rehearsed different scripts inside my head for the entire week. I would say things to myself like, 'Ah hello Cat, this is

Wendy, you know the woman who shot you in the arm.' Ah Cat it's been a long time, but I just wanted to say sorry I shot you....' Honestly, there was not going to be any easy way to get this done.

I decided I needed to treat the conversation like I was going into a store to buy a black dress and couldn't stop to buy anything else. Go in and get out. Don't linger. Be committed and take charge of the conversation.

When I finally picked up the phone I had to override the voices in my head that were telling me not to call. I punched in the phone number Max had given me long ago. It rang and rang and for a moment I thought I might get off the hook, until there was click and a faint, "Hello?" I was chilled by the sound of her voice. Her face flashed in my mind. Her long blond hair, the peek-a-boo bangs covering one eye. Memories flooded back. I had been living such an upside-down life then. Day had become my night. Bad was my good and wrong was my right. I was so off balance. I had teetered on the edge of insanity all the time.

I took a deep breath and said, "Is this Cat?"

"Yup... who's this?"

"Ah, ah... this is Wendy... you know, Max's ex-wife?" A tomb-like quiet descended on the other end of the phone.

"I'm calling... to say, ah, to say.... I'm sorry." I stumbled over my words.

More silence. I talked even faster.

"I was wrong for what I did. I mean... I had no business shooting you like I did. I'm usually not a violent person. I went to Catholic School and everything. It was all that speed I was doing. I don't want to make any excuses by any means, but, but, I had a psychotic break, or I never would have done that for sure." I sounded like a blubbering idiot. "Well, I'm sober now and I want to say I'm sorry for what I did. I'm really, really sorry I hurt you."

Had an alien hi-jacked my body? I wondered.

There was silence. Had she hung up?

A few seconds passed until finally Cat sighed and said, "It's okay...I'm sorry for some things I did as well."

I was sure I had heard her incorrectly. "It was certainly a crazy time for all of us..."

"It certainly was," she said.

The conversation did not go at all like I expected. She was supposed to tell me to fuck off or slam the phone down in my ear.

Trying to lighten-up the moment, I said, "I suppose I make a good argument for gun control."

A soft chuckle came from the other end.

"Well, thanks for taking my call...and take care, Cat."

"Yeah. You too."

After she hung up, I stared at the receiver in my hand. I had made the biggest amends of them all. I felt lighter somehow. It was then that I realized, with great clarity, how impossibly far I had come. I took a deep breath. It felt like I had dropped a huge boulder I didn't know I had been carrying, and now it was time to swim for the surface.

WOMAN FOUND DEAD IN TUB IN PARENTS' HOME

A Los Angeles housewife, Nancy Ely Adamson, 38, despondent over a pending divorce and possible loss other four children, apparently drowned herself in the bathtub in the Stockton home of her parents yesterday.

The woman's mother, Mrs. G. W. Ely, found her in the home at 1452 Oxford Way.

Coroner's deputies said Mrs. Adamson returned Tuesday night from Los Angeles where she had gone to talk with her attorney about a divorce hearing.

Mrs. Adamson was left alone in the house at 11 a.m. when her father left for work. Mrs. Ely had departed earlier.

Mrs. Ely found the house locked when she returned at 6 p.m. and broke through a window screen to find her daughter submerged in the water-filled tub. There was a deep cut on her left arm, apparently self inflicted as a razor blade was found in the bottom of the tub.

A suitcase contains her clothing was also in the bathtub with her.

Deputies said Mrs. Adamson and her husband, Douglas, of Beverly Hills had been separated. Both seeking custody of the four children.

The body was taken to the Young Memorial Chapel.

— Stockton News, 5/04/1960

Letting Go

After seven hours of driving I finally made it to the cemetery where my mother had been laid to rest. I sat in front of the black rod iron gates with my car engine ticking as if a bomb might go off inside. I had arrived early, allowing me more time to think about my mother's demise.

When I try really hard I can still conjure up images of her inside my mind. Her twinkling eyes, long elegant neck and the distinct way she threw her head back whenever she laughed. I can remember her tugging the knots out of my hair with a comb and the way she'd hold me on her lap to read me a bed time story at night. She could be so tender one minute, and the next all the signs of a loving mother would disappear.

Vanish.

Gone, without a trace.

For the first seven years of my life, a time when a child's brain is developing the needed skills to maintain healthy relationships, I was trying to survive. As a result, I became hyper-vigilant with my fight or flight reflexes actively engaged. No wonder I used drugs. I needed something to relax.

What the obituary failed to mention, was my mother stuffed photographs of her children inside that suitcase she pulled on top of her in the tub. Makes me shudder just to think about it.

How fucking tragic is that?

I'm brought back to the moment when a security guard dressed in a crisp black uniform comes to unlock the thick chain. He used the weight of his shoulder to open the heavy gate. After a taut nod of his head, I drove-in making my way through a long tunnel of magnolias. The sun shot pillars of light through a canopy of trees. A gust of wind sent brown leaves spiraling along the roadside. Head stones and crypts, like pop-tarts spread out in rows across the lush green lawns. At the end of the road was a six-foot mausoleum stood alone. I followed the map that I had printed at home and turned left, driving all the way to the chain link fence to park my car.

When I turned the ignition off, I closed my eyes for a moment and took a deep breath. Then I got out of the car and walked with my flip-flops snapping against the bottoms of my soles. I could tell this area was the low-rent district of the cemetery with its concrete slabs to mark the graves instead of the traditional headstones. When I got to the curb I counted five graves in and froze when I saw my mother's name etched in a stone embedded in moist almond-colored dirt: *Nancy Adamson 1922 to 1960*. A lump formed in the back of my throat, my hand reached for a letter that I had brought. I looked both ways to make sure no one was watching me me before reading it out loud:

Dearest Mom,

It's taken me a while to get here to pay my respects because I was resentful.

For so long I missed having a mother and was profoundly sad, but no one talked about you after you left.

I wish you could have been there in my teenage years. I wish you could have been there at my wedding day. I wish you could have been there when I was pregnant, and when I gave birth to my two boys. I wish you could have watched them grow up into the men they are today. You would be so proud of who they've become. I certainly am.

Every single thing in my life, large and small, has echoed with the absence of not having a mother by my side. But I want you to know that I'm okay now.

Getting sober was the hardest, yet, the best thing that ever happened to me. It forced me to reconcile things I was holding on to. It seems that if I want to be truly free, I had to let you off the hook. And so, Mom, I've come here to say I'm not angry anymore and want you to know, I love you very, very much.

Your Daughter Forever...

Afterward, a soft rush or air escaped my lips. I stuffed the letter in my jean pocket. As I turned to leave I wasn't struck by a lightning bolt, there wasn't a burning bush or a chariot in the sky, but I did realize that in order to change the trajectory of my families lineage, I would not only have to forgive others, I would have to forgive myself.

Epilogue

In the fifties, Venice, California was known for its beatniks with their black turtlenecks, berets, dark glasses and poetry slams. These nonconformists were eventually replaced by the pot-smoking, acid-tripping hippies of the sixties. By the seventies, the junkies slithered in and although we were everywhere, the average Joe might not realize it because we were sneaking down back alleys, ducking into doorways at the sight of a patrol car, and sleeping in roach-infested shooting galleries. But in 2015, Venice, where 'the debris meets the sea,' had turned into a major tourist spot. That's where I was that early Thanksgiving morning, doing my best to stay warm with a cup of Starbucks clutched in my hands.

A roller bladder with arms swinging like pendulums, zipped by in a blur, just as Rikki pulled up in his Ford Explorer.

"Happy Thanksgiving, Mom!" he yelled out his window.

"Happy Thanksgiving." I waved.

He pulled onto the edge of the basketball courts and opened the back of his car, revealing trash bags full of sneakers. Retrieving one of the Hefty bags, he threw it over his shoulder to get started setting up his booth.

To fully understand why we were there, I need to go back to when Becky bought Rikki those two pair of Vans more than twenty years before. Although Rikki never forgot Becky's kindness, his early deprivation would turn him into a sneaker head, with a collection of more than a hundred and fifty pairs of tennis shoes climbing up his bedroom wall.

I first became aware of the sneaker culture back in the 80's when Nike used celebrity branding to give kids prestige on the playground. A lot of times a sneaker's coolness is related to how many people can get their hands on them. And while Rikki got his hands on hundreds of sneakers through the years, he seemed to be lacking any real direction in his life.

As Rikki struggled through his twenties, I was becoming increasingly worried about him. By his early thirties, Rikki, was having his own bottoming-out of sorts when he felt empty and lost.

One morning he called me bright and early. "Mom, I was tossing and turning all night because I couldn't sleep. All of the sudden, I bolted straight up in my bed and looked over at all my shoes stacked against my wall." He let out a long sigh. "I had to ask myself what am I doing with all those shoes? I don't even wear most of them and there are people out there that don't have any at all. So, I've made a decision to give them away."

MY first thought was he'd probably regret it later, but I kept my mouth shut. Instead, I asked, "Who are you giving them to?"

"I'm not sure yet, but I'm sure there's someone out there who could use a pair."

Later that same morning, Rikki loaded up his car and drove the streets of L.A. until he gave away his first pair of shoes to a homeless man. As a photographer, Rikki took a before and after photo, and posted it on social media. His followers loved the idea and many of them wanted to donate their shoes. Rikki had found his purpose and started a grass roots organization, and called it Hav A Sole. Since that first day, he has given out thousands of shoes to those in need.

On this particular morning, we had joined forces with other non-profits who were there to feed the homeless. People were setting out turkeys, mashed potatoes and stuffing on banquet tables that lined all the way to the end of the basketball courts. Another table had blessing bags filled with basic needs items.

A line of people had already started wrapping around the basketball courts. Rikki and his volunteers had already set up the Hav A Sole booth when a girl, dressed in a pink chiffon skirt and a scarf hugging her hips walked up.

"You giving out shoes?" she queried.

"What size do you wear?" I asked.

"A size nine."

"I like the outfit you're wearing."

"I do belly dancing on the boardwalk."

"I'm sure you could use something with support?"

"I am always on my feet."

I scanned the rows of shoes until I found a pair of pink Nikes and held them up. "How about these?"

"Oh…I like those a lot." A sweet smile lit up her face.

"I'm sure you can do some serious belly dancing in these." I handed them to her.

"Thank you so much," she said, before rolling away on her skateboard.

The first time I went with Rikki and gave away a pair of shoes, I was hooked. It was simple, it was direct, there was an obvious need, and the process created a level of intimacy between myself and the recipient that was so satisfying I started volunteering all the time.

As it started to warm, sweat beaded-up on the back of my neck. I took off my sweatshirt and tied it around my waist. All around people moved like extras on a movie set. Some were eating, some sifted through piles of donated clothes, while others stood in long lines waiting their turn. A group of animated street kids spoke to one other, nodding and flicking their cigarettes.

After an hour or so, I spotted my nine-year-old grandson, Matthew, running toward me. "Grandma, we're here."

"Hi Sweetie," I folded him into my arms.

"Look, Dad's coming over there." He reached around and pointed to the other side of the basketball court. My gaze landed on Jerry, Erika and Max who was walking a lot slower these days. Out in front were three more of my grandchildren, ages ranging from nine to eighteen. They had all come to help donate shoes.

"Happy Thanksgiving Mom." Jerry gave me a bear hug.

"Happy Thanksgiving."

I was so proud of who Jerry had become. He was a devoted father who had been transformed through parenting his own kids.

I turned to Max. "How are you feeling these days?" I asked.

"Old." He shrugged. "But I guess there's nothing we can do about that."

"We can't stay sixteen forever..."

An elderly woman, with-beaten skin shuffled by clutching several shopping bags in her fist.

Max nodded at the rows of sneakers underneath the canopy. "So, this is what Rikki's been up to lately?"

"Yup. This is Hav A Sole." I nodded.

"Where do all these shoes come from?"

"Most of them come from local Nike stores who donate their returned shoes to us."

We gazed over at Rikki, a few yards away in a baseball cap, handing out a pair of blue and white pair of sneakers to a home-less teen in baggy khaki shorts. Jerry, Erika, and my grandkids started helping out as well.

Max shook his head. "I guess our boys turned-out alright after all."

A smile pushed across my face. I sighed softly. "Yup. They sure did. And that's something I'm grateful for every day."

Acknowledgments

To all the people who believed in me and saw something that I was unable to see in myself, thank you from the bottom of my heart. I had no defense against your kindness and you cracked my heart wide open.

I want to thank Karin Gutman, Patricia Verducci, Shawney Kelley, Kelly Hartog, Molly Jordan for all your feedback. It helped me to want to become a better writer.

I am deeply grateful to my little writing group in Topanga, The Vulnerables. A magical time and place that I still miss today.

Thank you to Kristen Johnson for your brilliant edits.

I want to especially thank Paul Hook for always being supportive and believing in me.

Thank you to all of you who wrote blurbs for my book. Your words meant so much.

Thank you to Rob Cohen and Christine Roth for believing in this book.

Lastly, and most importantly, I want to thank my boys, Jerry and Rikki. For the record, I'm so incredibly proud of both of you. Thank you for teaching me what it takes to be a mother.

I love you very much.

CPSIA information can be obtained
at www.ICGtesting.com
Printed in the USA
LVHW042252200519
618457LV00025B/845